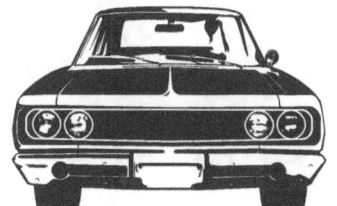 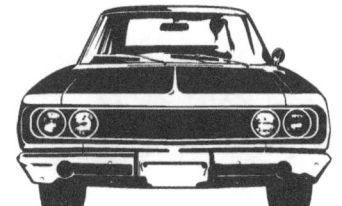

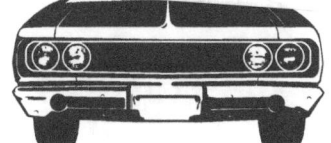

The Greatest American Cars Coloring Book - Pro Edition

Alexander Watts

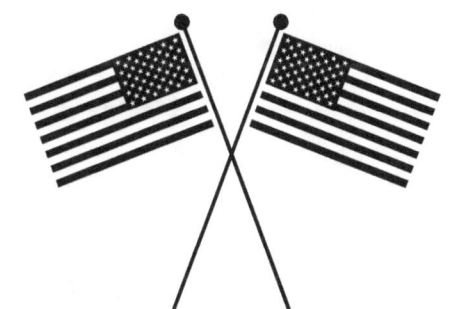 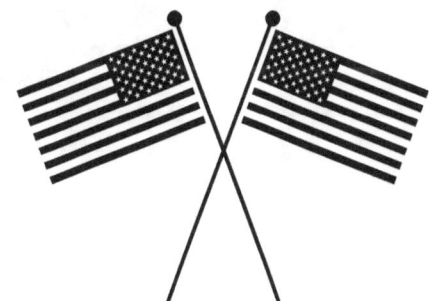

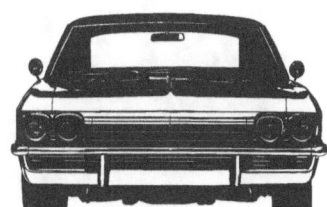 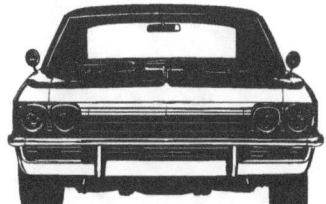 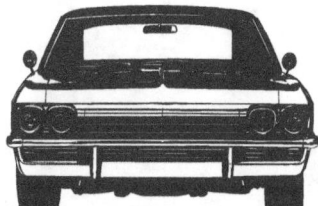

The Greatest American Cars Coloring Book

by

Alexander Watts

Introduction: America's emotive automobiles

Hello, and welcome to *The Greatest American Cars Coloring Book*, the latest edition of the very successful coloring book series by Amazon Best Selling Author Alexander Watts!

This book presents a journey, from the beginnings of the first American automotive icons through to the modern wonders of today.

It all began with the Industrial Revolution in Britain, Europe and then America between 1760 and 1840. New industrial processes started an era of exponential invention and manufacturing expansion – and changed everything in a world economy previously built on farming, hunting and fishing. Across the planet, slow and primitive transport networks couldn't support the new, more fluent world of international trade. So, turnpike road systems, canals and railway networks were developed to deliver raw materials to the new factories, and then get their finished products out to world markets, quickly and cost effectively.

The American automotive industry rode high on the crest of this wave too. Although the first automobile was patented in 1886 in Germany by Carl Benz with his "Vehicle Powered By A Gas Engine"— by 1904 European designs began to be overtaken as the USA developed mass production lines rolling out more affordable American cars to a mass market. It wasn't plain sailing though. In the early years the new American industry was a mess, with about 45 different car companies. Each company sold only in small numbers. Many went out of business between the day a customer ordered a car and the day it was due to be delivered. This became known as "manufacturer gambling", and it created a major lack of confidence in the marketplace.

To build consumer confidence back up again, industrialist Benjamin Briscoe proposed amalgamating all the main car companies into one superpower. This would merge the powers of Ford, REO (Ransom E Olds), his own company Maxwell-Briscoe and Buick (created by William Crapo Durant). Briscoe's idea didn't appeal to either Ford or REO, but was approved by Durant of Buick. And so was born the true automotive giant General Motors (GM). GM went on to build the conglomerate by taking in other auto manufacturers like Oldsmobile (struggling after Ransom Olds departed), Cadillac, and Oakland (which was soon to become Pontiac).

By the 1920s three giants dominated the US automotive industry. "The Big Three" comprised The Ford Motor Company, General Motors and Chrysler. In the late 1930s through to 1945 there was a combined focus on winning WWII, with The Big Three funneling their resources into the military effort. After the war it took some years before the industry came to resemble how we know it today. With models proliferating and technological development making giant strides, car makers began loading vehicles with increasingly expensive, new and improved gadgets. The economic theory was that bigger cars were more profitable than smaller ones – a truism that has prevailed right up to today.

The American auto industry proved to be a leading force of change in the 20th century. In its prime in the 1980s it provided employment to one in every six Americans. Over 80% of the US population had a vehicle, and 50% of people had access to two. With the vast geographical area of this nation and the huge diversity of its economy and society, the USA was always going to fall in love with the car and depend on it mightily. Quite literally, they were made for each other!

So, this leads me on to America's finest and greatest ever cars — a rich and glorious heritage. It was extremely difficult to whittle them down to the 32 in this coloring book when there were so many to consider – cars with huge amounts of power that are super-fast; cars that defined an era and influenced automotive design the world over; cars that will remain forever in the hearts of those who were lucky enough to own them.

These are the cars that are truly loved by Americans. These are the Greatest ever American Cars of all time.

THE GREATEST AMERICAN CARS COLORING BOOK COLOR TEST PAGE

Table of Contents

The daddy of them all... Any color you want, as long as it's black (or, gray, blue, green or red!).

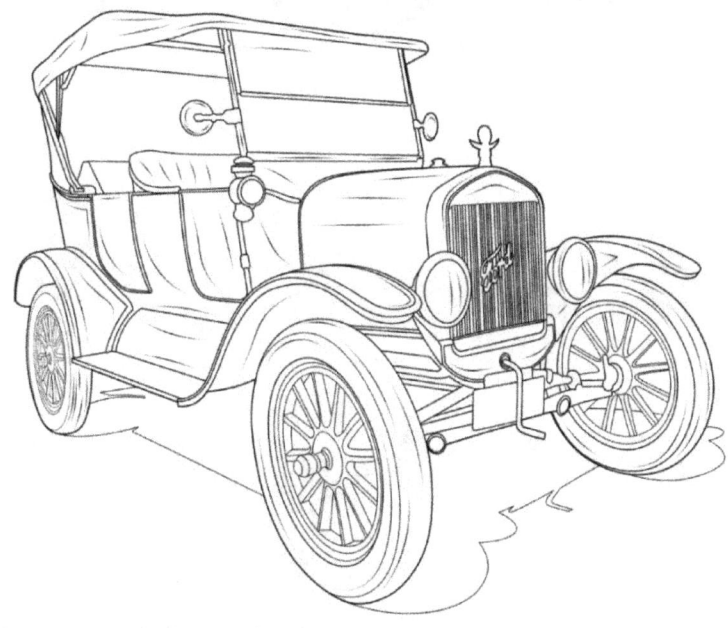

Ford Model T (1908-1927)

Colloquially known as "Tin Lizzie" or "Leaping Lena", the Ford Model T is, possibly, the most influential car of the 20th century – the first of its kind to offer inexpensive transportation on a universal scale. It changed the landscape of the American automotive industry.

Okay, so it may not have been the fastest car in history or the most stylish. But the Ford Model T was the most revolutionary car of its time and was widely regarded as the first automobile for the ordinary middle-class American. This was because The Model T was Ford's first mass-produced automobile, allowing it to get rid of expensive and inefficient hand-built production techniques. It quickly became a symbol of the United States' age of modernization.

Henry Ford was once famously reported as telling his management team: "Any customer can have a car painted in any color that he wants – so long as it's black!". This was true, but only between 1914 and 1926 – a one-color production line kept manufacturing costs down. But at its launch in 1908 the car had been available in gray, green, blue and red.

Model illustrated:	1925 Ford Model T Touring
Power:	20 hp
Engine:	177 cu.i. (cubic inches) / 2,900cc inline 4-cylinder gasoline with RWD
Weight:	1,650 lbs / 748 kg
0-60:	n/a
Top Speed:	45 mph
Numbers Produced:	15 million (approx.)

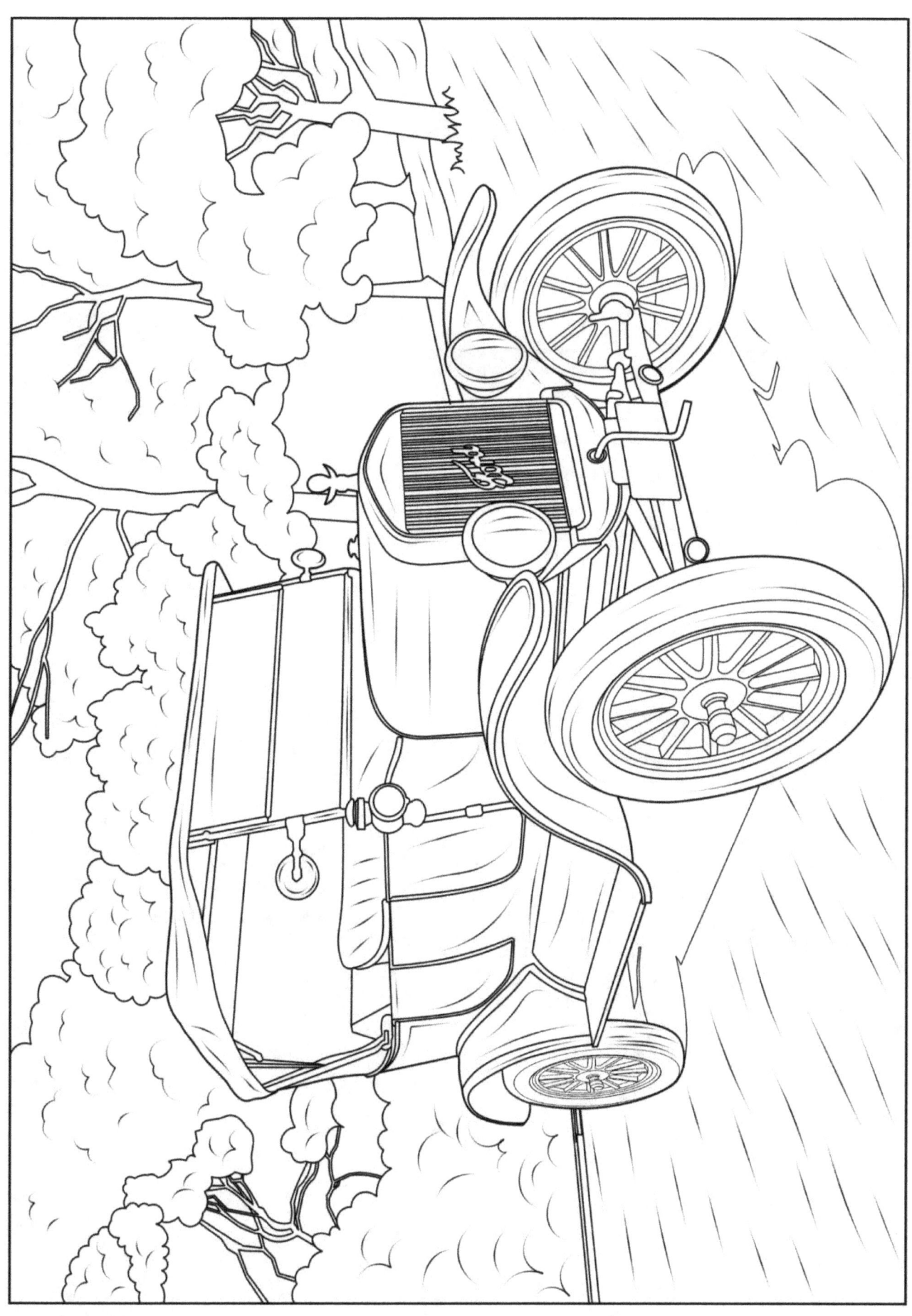

What a Duesy! King of the Indy 500, then Emperor of American luxury.

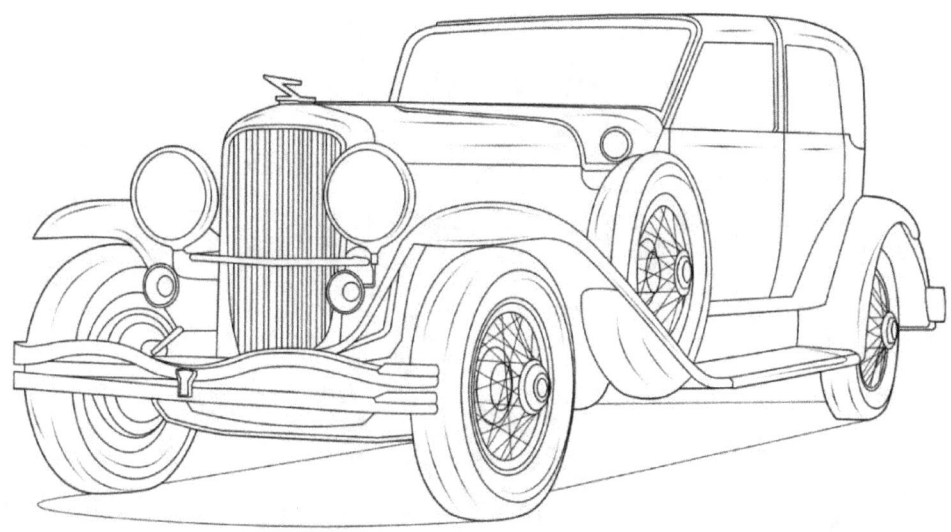

Duesenberg Model J (1928-1937)

Fred and Augie Duesenberg were German-American brothers who, in 1913, set up the Minnesota-based Duesenberg Motors Company Inc. They were self-taught engineers who specialized in building race engines. Duesenberg cars – known as "Duesys" – were all hand built and rated among the finest vehicles in the world.

Duesenberg first tasted racing success when Edward (Eddie) Rickenbacker drove one into 10th place in the 1914 Indianapolis 500. They built on this and in the next decade they dominated the Indy 500 with four wins in six years — 1922, 1924, 1925 and 1927.

In 1925 the Duesenberg company was bought out by respected businessman Errett Cord, who went on to become a transport industry leader for a large part of the 20th century. Bringing new direction, Cord set out to produce the biggest, fastest, most powerful and luxurious car in the world. He aimed to rival the likes of Mercedes-Benz, Rolls-Royce, Hispano-Suiza, Isotta-Fraschini and Minerva, who were all producing impressive grand touring cars during that era. Cord's work resulted in the Duesenberg Model J (pictured above) – America's fastest and most powerful production vehicle at the time.

The exclusive Model J Duesy proved a game changer for the American elite – the very antithesis of the more common Fords and Chevrolets of the day.

Model illustrated:	1930 Duesenberg Model J Sport Berline
Power:	265 hp (non-supercharged variant)
Engine:	420 cu.i. (6,876cc) DOHC straight-eight gasoline with RWD
Weight:	5,269lbs / 2,390 kg
0-60:	13 seconds
Top Speed:	119 mph
Numbers Produced:	480 (approx. incl. SJ, SSL, & JN models)

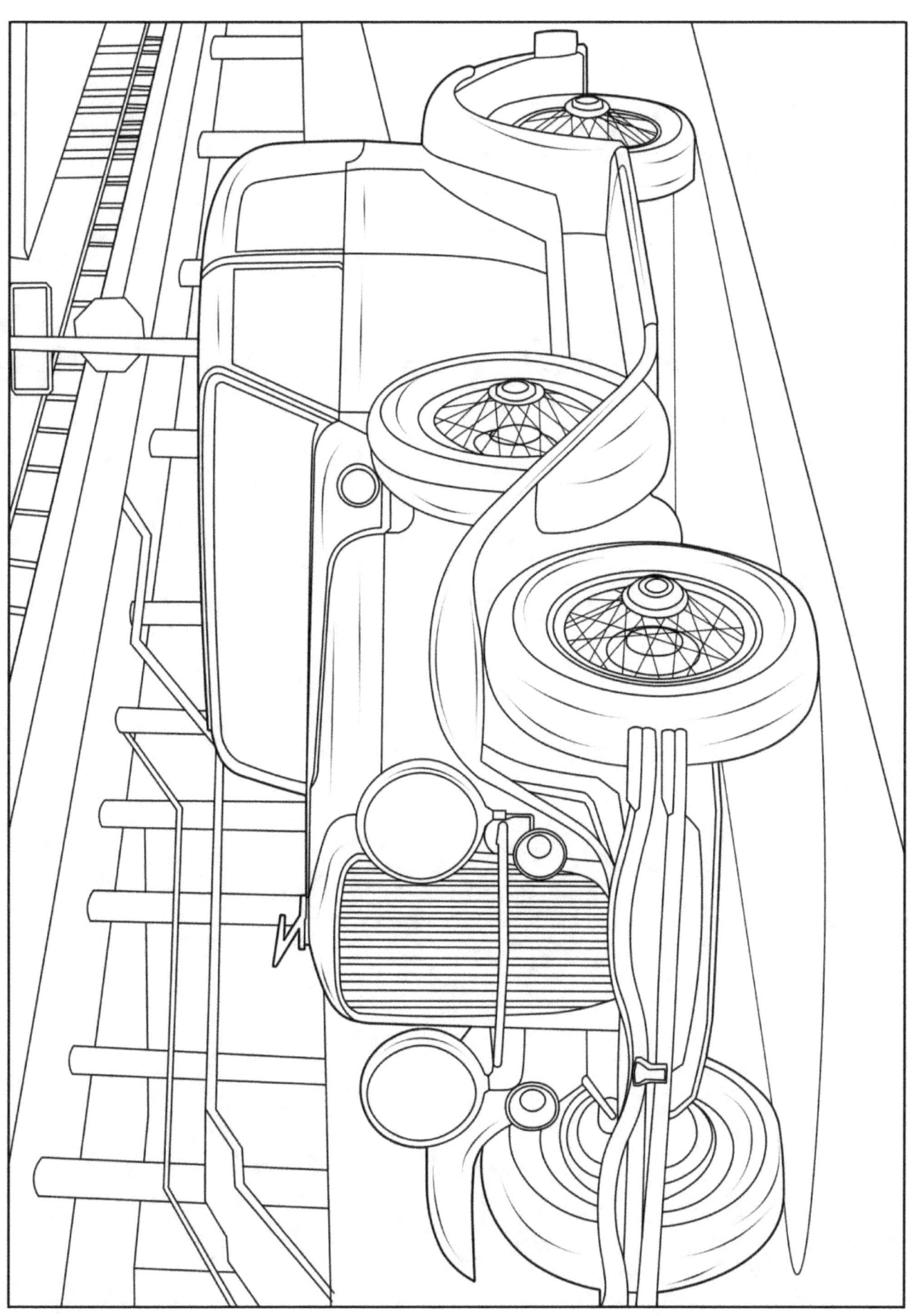

Smooth, classy, personalized....
With a monster lurking under the hood.

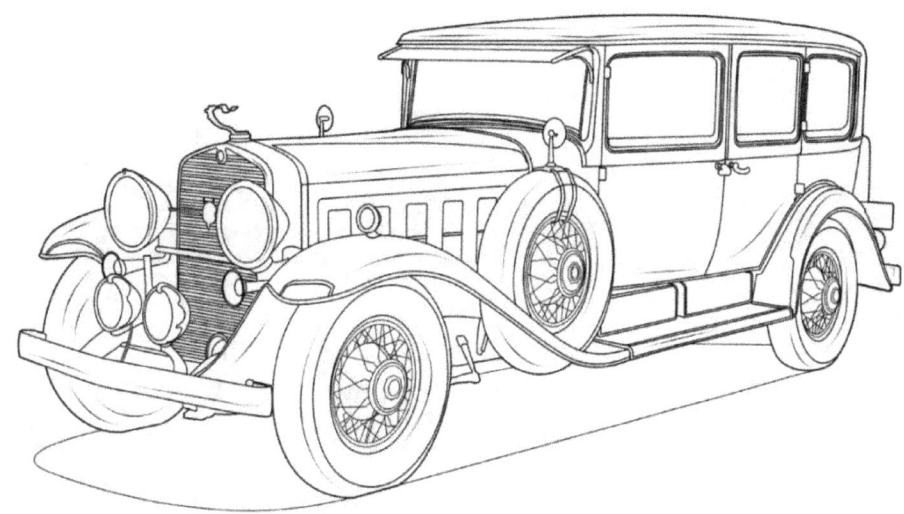

Cadillac V16 (1930-1940)

Not wishing just to surpass its rivals with more regular power plants like V8s, V10s and somewhat pedestrian V12s, Cadillac set out to produce a car with a cylinder count that really was different – a V16. It was effectively two straight-eight engines sharing a common crankshaft and crankcase, with two single-barrel carburetors. This was a significant technical challenge at the time, but it reflected Cadillac's pre-war status as a world pioneer in automotive luxury and technology. Its priority was to produce a smooth, quality and classy vehicle that exuded sheer class from every angle.

The monster of an engine was fitted to a complete monster of a car. Its wheelbase was a very significant 148 inches (12-feet, four inches/3.76 meters, later extended to 154 inches/12-feet, 10 inches/3.91 meters) which was, again, unheard of at the time. Sales of this "halo" Cadillac car were initially good, making up a significant 20 percent of all Cadillac's sales despite the impact of the Great Depression.

Each V16 was built to the individual customer's specification, with each chassis being sent to Fleetwood in Pennsylvania for final completion. A choice of around 70 different body styles were available, all extremely elaborate, highly individualized and exquisitely finished. For a car that was immensely expensive it survived well. Sales were buoyant until 1933, when the Great Depression really began to hit the economy and impact the affordability of such a grand vehicle. The Cadillac V16 is a car that made a lasting mark.

Model illustrated: 1930 Cadillac V16 Fleetwood Imperial
Power: 165-185 hp
Engine: 452 cu.i. (7,410cc) V16 gasoline with RWD
Weight: 6,199 lbs / 2,812 kg
0-60:   24 seconds
Top Speed: 90 mph
Numbers Produced: 4,076

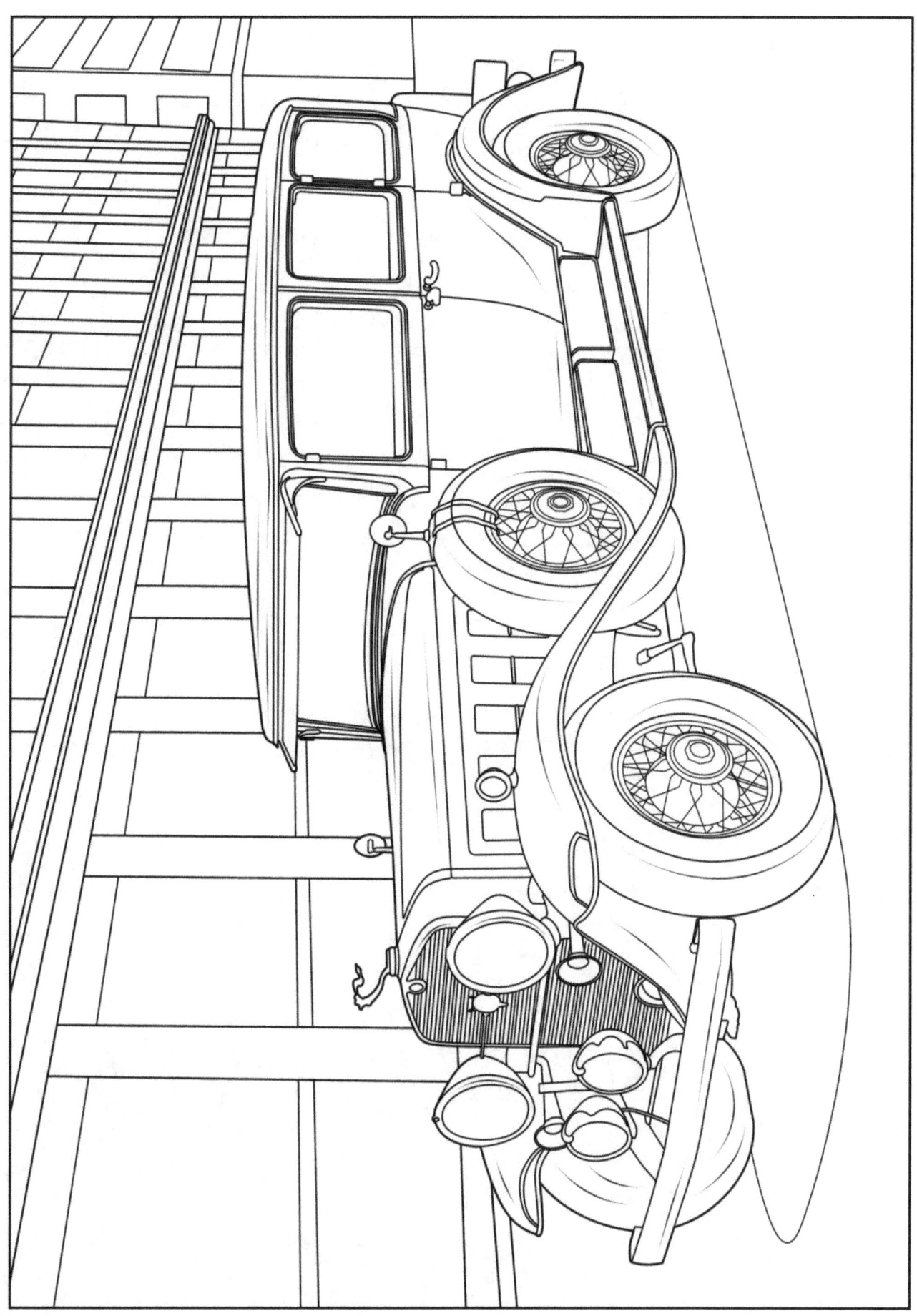

Back to the future, literally…
Reversing through traffic in the streets of Detroit!

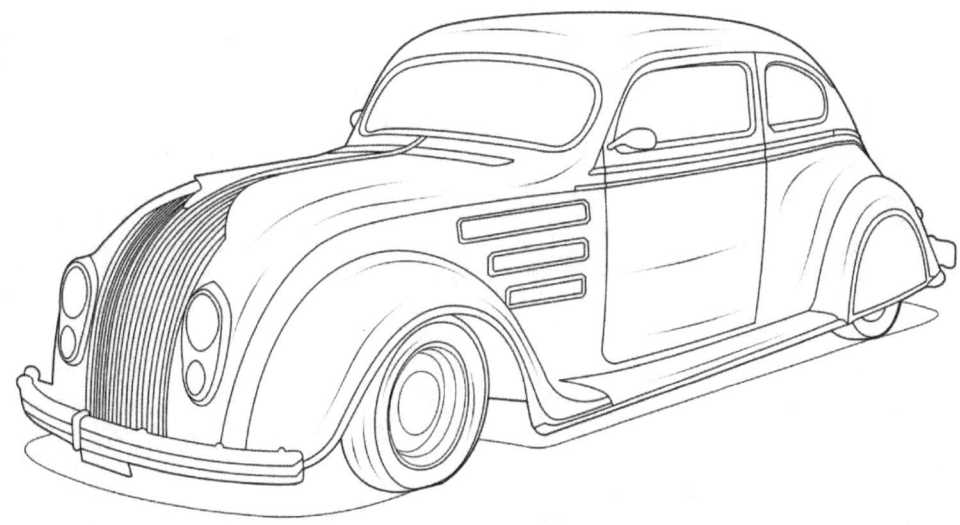

Chrysler Airflow (1934–1937)

Although in sales numbers it wasn't the car that the Chrysler Corporation hoped for, the controversial Chrysler Airflow is one is the most influential cars in American history. It featured flowing curves, long horizontal lines and various nautical elements, hugely influenced by the Art Deco and "Streamline Moderne" movements. This made it one of the most advanced cars of its generation – and Chrysler wasn't afraid to advertise it as such. The Airflow introduced many innovations, such as a unibody construction, hydraulic brakes, double-glazed windows, aerodynamically considered body styling (using a wind tunnel for the first time), and a multitude of safety features and luxurious interior details.

Chrysler wanted everyone to know it was onto something big. So, to hit the headlines and pinpoint its rivals' lack of aerodynamic styling, Chrysler actually reversed the axles and steering gear on a regular model and then drove backwards through the streets of Detroit!

The Airflow was Chrysler's attempt to set itself apart from the competition, but sadly the attempt failed in the marketplace. This led Chrysler to take a significantly more conservative design path with future models. Nevertheless, the Airflow's iconic styling and features influenced car design for many years to come.

Model illustrated:	1934 Chrysler Airflow 2 Door Coupe
Power:	117 hp
Engine:	323 cu.i. (5,301 cc) straight eight gasoline with RWD
Weight:	3,927 lbs / 1,781 kg
0-60:	Circa 20 seconds
Top Speed:	90 mph
Numbers Produced:	55,000 (approx.)

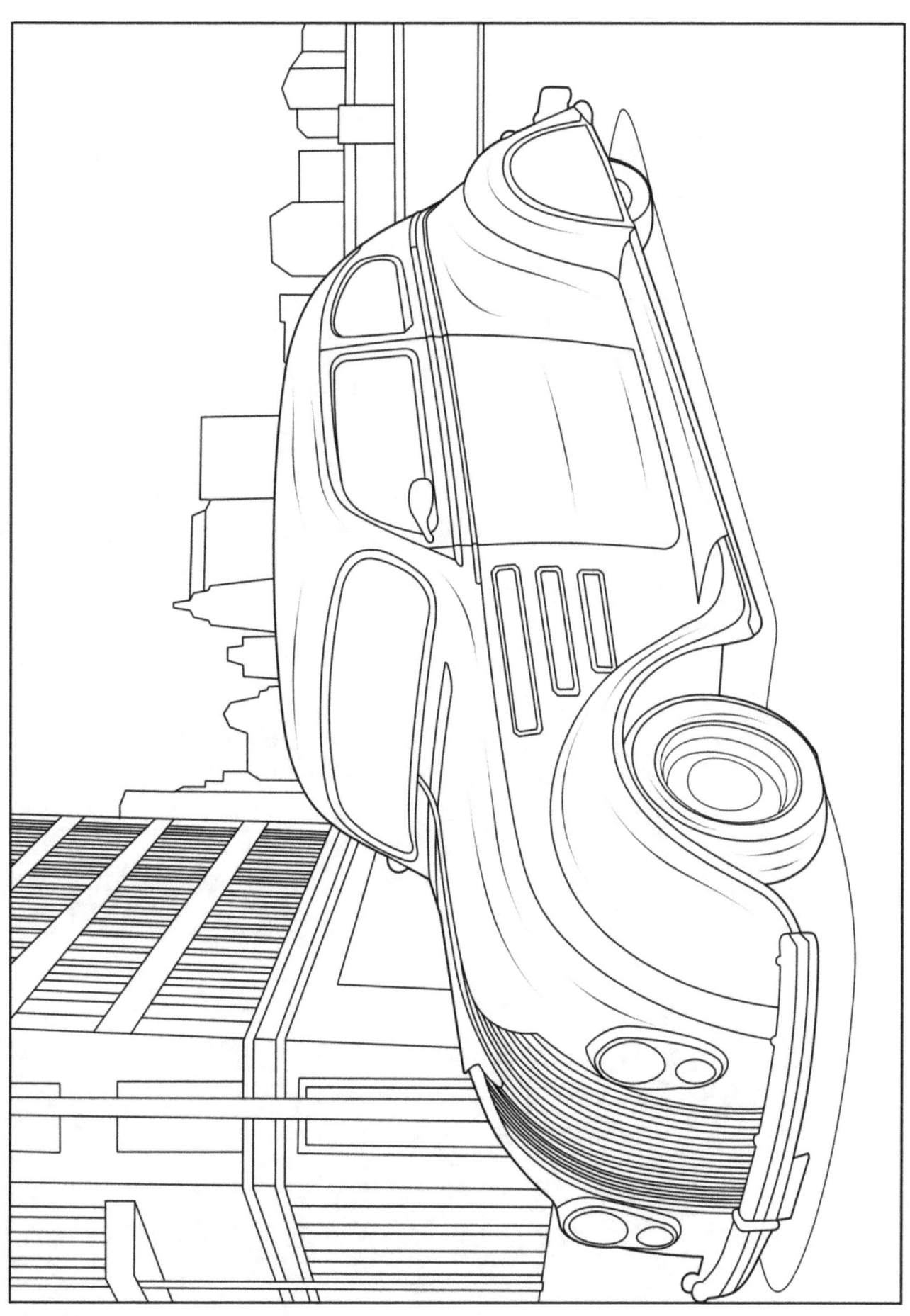

Take a half-ton truck, add windows all round, and cook up an original people carrier.

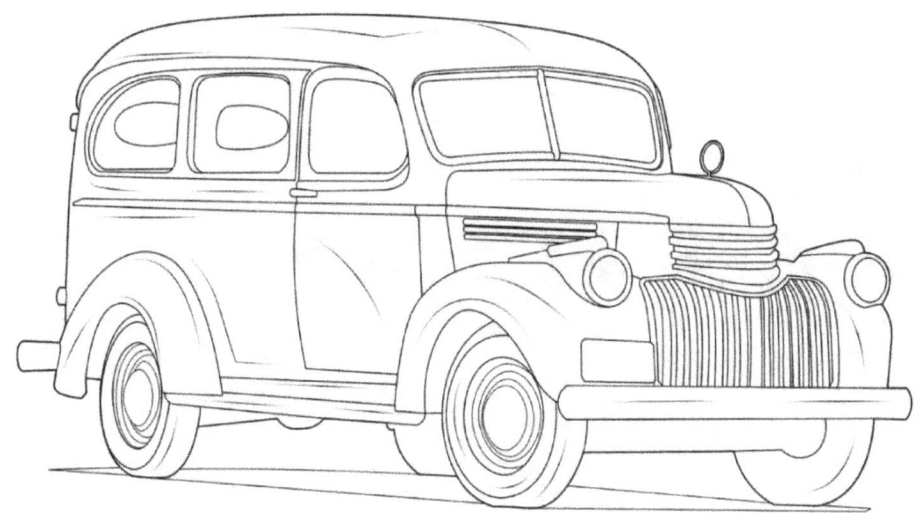

Chevrolet Suburban (1935-Present)

You know a recipe doesn't need adjustment when it's as successful as the Suburban has been - its 80 years in showrooms is the longest unbroken production cycle in history, and it's still going strong.

Originally called the Suburban Carryall, this tough, no-nonsense load carrier was the first all metal-bodied station wagon. Its initial frame was fundamentally a windowed body set atop a half-ton truck chassis. It was the first of its kind – a car that defined a new breed of "people carrier", and the forerunner of today's SUVs.

From its very humble commercial beginnings, the Chevy Suburban evolved over its more than eight decades to the 12-generation behemoth which today still transports modern American families in absolute comfort on their daily commutes. It's no wonder Chevrolet claims it to be one of America's most defining vehicles.

Model illustrated:	Third Generation 1946 Chevrolet Suburban
Power:	90 hp
Engine:	216.5 cu.i. (3,800 cc) inline six gasoline with RWD
Weight:	3,400 lbs / 1,542 kg
0-60:	Not recorded
Top Speed:	Not recorded
Numbers Produced:	2,000,000+ (approx. across all generations)

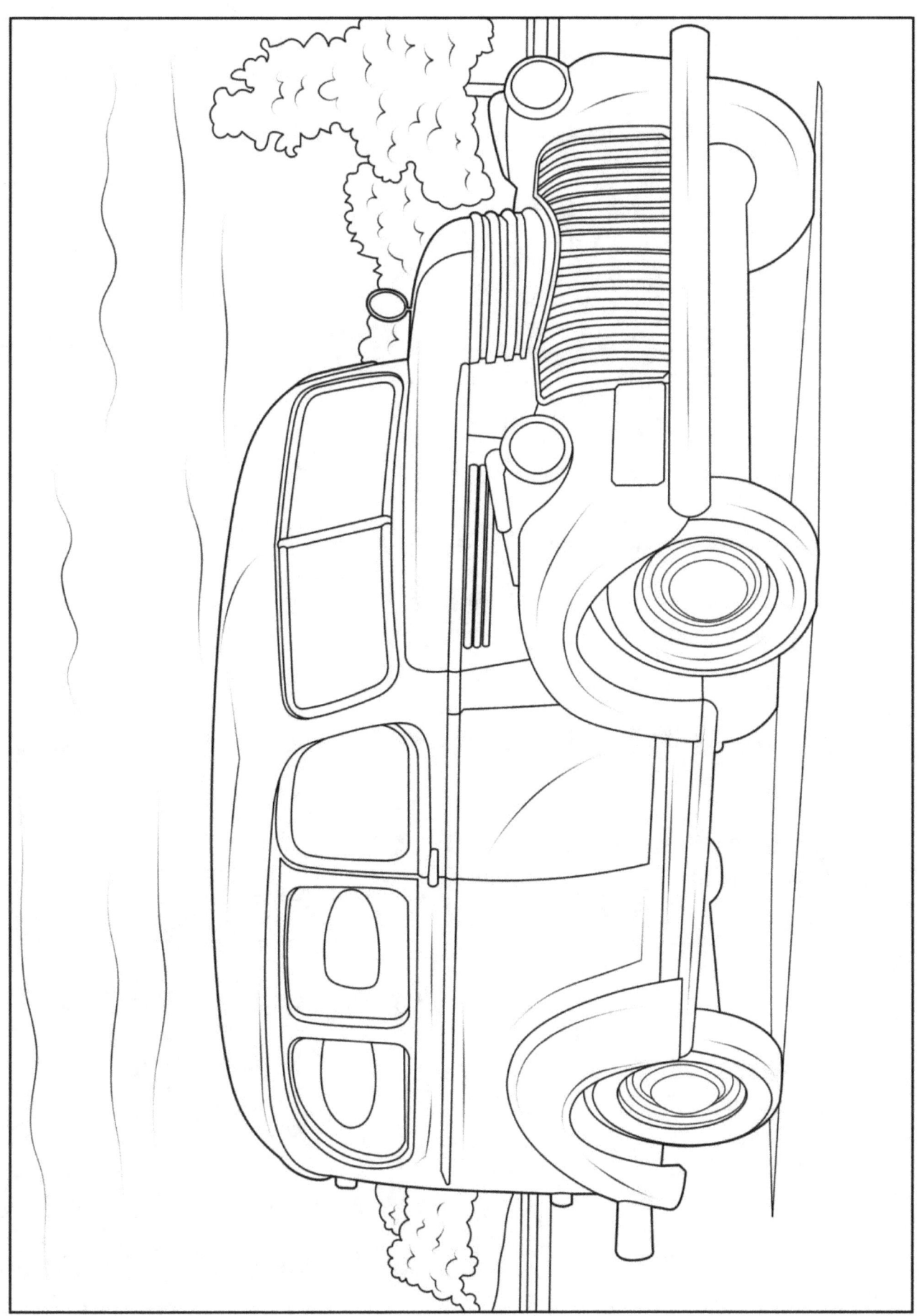

Most famous for the wrong reason:
Luxurious Lincoln's infamous icon.

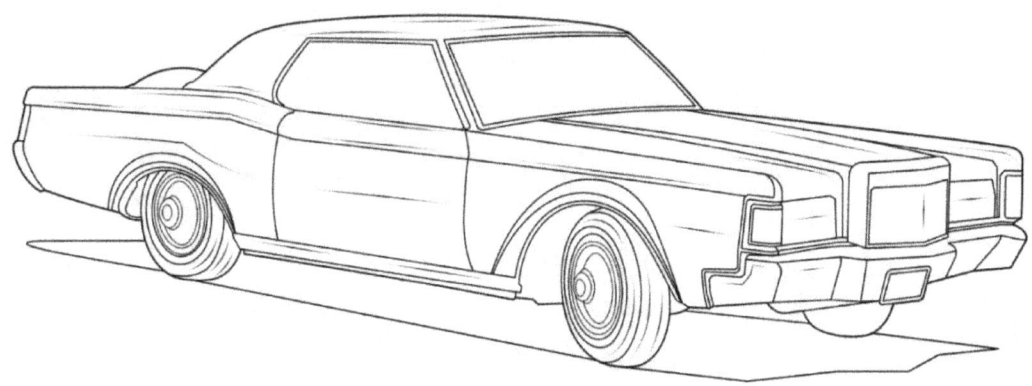

Lincoln Continental (1939-1948, 1956-2002, 2016-Present)

Thanks mainly to its rather wonderful Continental sedan, first seen in 1961, Ford subsidiary Lincoln enjoyed considerable success throughout the 1960s. The '61 was significant as it focused Lincoln's efforts onto a more personal, luxurious market – a sector it has inhabited for the majority of its existence.

This market focus led to some notable luxury cars. Sadly, the most famous of all was President John. F. Kennedy's open-top '61 Lincoln Continental 4 Door Convertible Limousine used for his tragic motorcade through Dealey Plaza, Dallas, Texas, when he was assassinated on November 22nd, 1963. He was the eighth president to die in office and the fourth to be assassinated.

The Mark III Coupe was, perhaps, one of the finest looking and most graceful of all Continentals, designed to compete against Cadillac's impressive Eldorado. Underneath the Mark III Coupe's hood sat a gargantuan 460 cubic-inch V8 engine delivering performance that can politely be classed only as 'moderate'. Fuel economy was a measly 10 miles per gallon if you went light on the gas pedal. The car featured many interesting details such as hideaway headlights, vinyl roof and a hump on the trunk to house the spare wheel – with the car's insignia emblazoned across it. It deployed a huge presence on the road – one of the many reasons that the Continental Mark III is rated among the finest personal luxury vehicles of its era.

Model illustrated:	1969 Lincoln Continental Mark III Coupe
Power:	365 hp
Engine:	460 cu.i. (7,536 cc) naturally aspirated eight-cylinder gasoline with RWD
Weight:	4,900 lbs / 2,222 kg
0-60:	9 seconds
Top Speed:	125 mph
Numbers Produced:	80,000 (approx.)

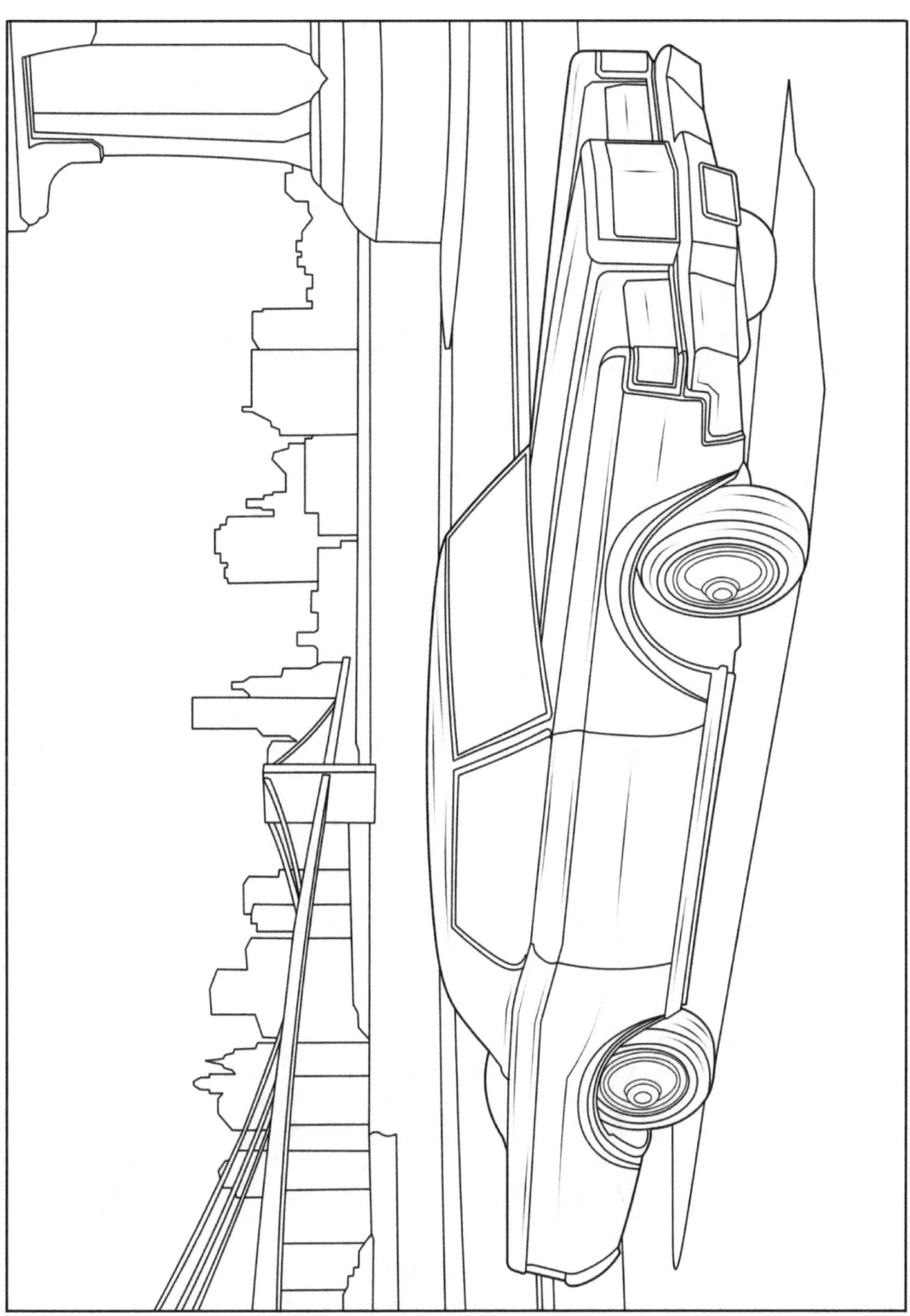

Military trailblazer which created the civilian off-road car market.

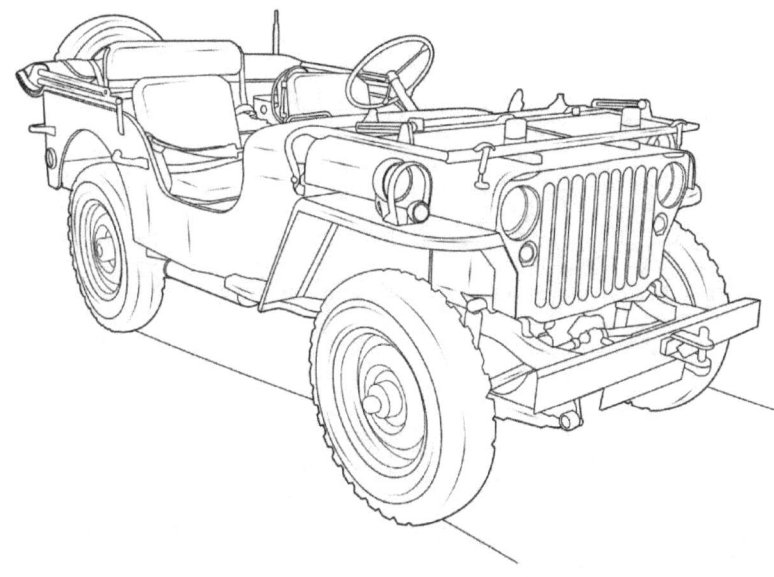

Willys Jeep (1941-1946)

From 1912-1918 Willys Overland Motor Company was the second largest producer of vehicles, just behind the immensely powerful Ford Motor Company. Although things weren't easy for Willys during the post-Depression era of the 1930s, it (along with Ford and American Bantam) was awarded the contract for production of a lightweight truck to help with the WWII war effort.

The requirement was to supply a military vehicle capable of crossing any terrain and withstanding bullets and explosions in suboptimal conditions. How it became known as a Jeep from its multiple manufacturers is argued by historians. But one explanation is that when production started in 1941, just before the US entered WWII, the Army referred to it as a "G.P." ("General Purpose" or "Government Purpose"). And why say two-syllable "G-P" when one-syllable "Jeep" rolls off the tongue? Despite other manufacturers of the Army's Jeeps, Willys applied to trademark the Jeep name in 1943 and after several refusals the Patent Office granted it the invaluable trademark in 1950.

However it got its name, the Jeep's winning formula was to offer a simple 4WD layout, compact size, extremely rugged and very capable off-road performance. US General Dwight D. Eisenhower, Supreme Allied Commander in WWII and later President of the USA, reportedly wrote that most senior officers rated the Jeep as one of their top five war-winning pieces of equipment.

After WWII, production of the Jeep continued, both by Willys and by Ford, and it continued to be used in the Korean War. But Willys separately stripped off its military features and fully civilianized the Jeep, with the significant addition of a tailgate and side-mounted spare wheel, which evolved it into the Willys CJ-2A. These were initially intended as an alternative to farm tractors, which were in short supply due to lack of production during the war.

Ultimately, a total of 600,000 Willys Jeeps were produced and the 1945 version was the first mass-produced 4WD civilian vehicle. The rugged, compact off-road design inspired wide imitation over the years by manufacturers around the world, producing other 4WD and SUV vehicles, and Willys civilian Jeep introduced the term "4WD" as a common household phrase. The original Jeeps created a significant automotive legacy. Among all iconic cars, Jeeps are certainly one of the frontrunners.

Model illustrated:	1943 Willys Jeep
Power:	60 hp
Engine:	134 cu.i. (2,199 cc) four-cylinder gasoline with four-wheel drive (4WD)
Weight:	3,650 lbs / 1,655 kg
0-60:	22.8 seconds
Top Speed:	65 mph
Numbers Produced:	600,000+ (approx.)

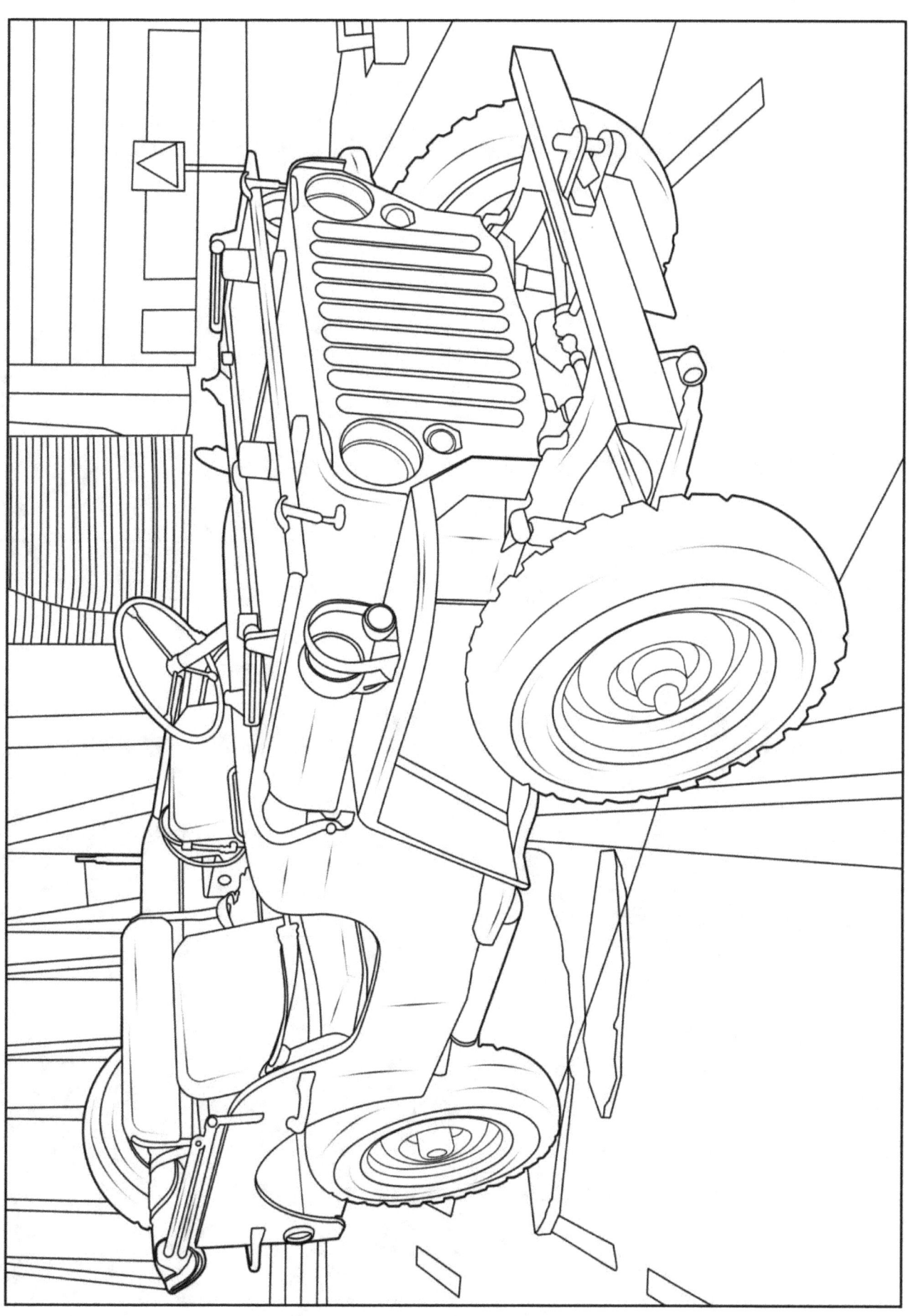

Out in front: after a record 35m sales, and outselling all the others into its 8th decade.

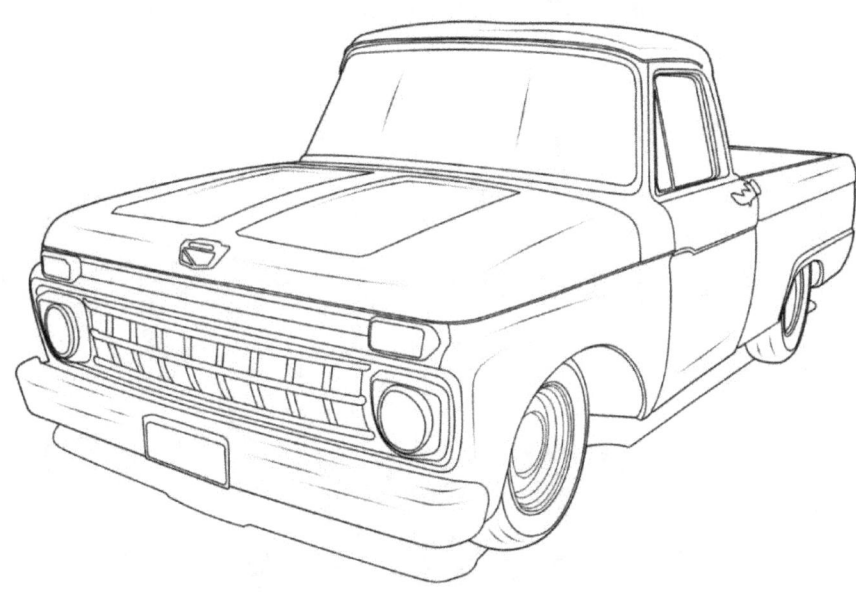

Ford F-Series Pickup (1948-Present)

Racking up its 14th generation with the 2021 model, the F-Series Pickup has been the biggest-selling pickup truck in the US since 1977. And no vehicle has outsold it overall in America since 1981! It's also been marketed as the Mercury M-Series.

Pickups are the only car class to successfully stand the test of time. Their format hasn't changed for over 100 years and they've cemented themselves as one of the backbones of economies across the world. Of the wide variety of models on offer across the country, one stands head and shoulders above the rest – the Ford F-Series.

Introduced in 1948 as the F-100, the F-Series has evolved gracefully from the original rugged workhorse to today's range of hugely comfortable and powerful models. A number of special edition models along the way has helped maintain customer interest – not that interest has ever been lacking in its rich 70+-year history. Today's F-Series trucks are high-tech machines that span the spectrum from work truck to luxury cruiser and are a true expression of Americana. With the F-Series' popularity as strong as it ever was, and sales figures continuing to dominate into an eighth decade, it's likely the F-Series will remain the automotive frontrunner for many years to come.

Model illustrated:	1961 (Fourth Generation) F100 F-Series Pickup
Power:	137 hp
Engine:	223 cu.i. (3,654 cc) inline six-cylinder gasoline with RWD
Weight:	3,384 lbs / 1,535 kg
0-60:	24 seconds (approx.)
Top Speed:	60-65 mph
Numbers Produced:	35,000,000+ (approx. across all generations)

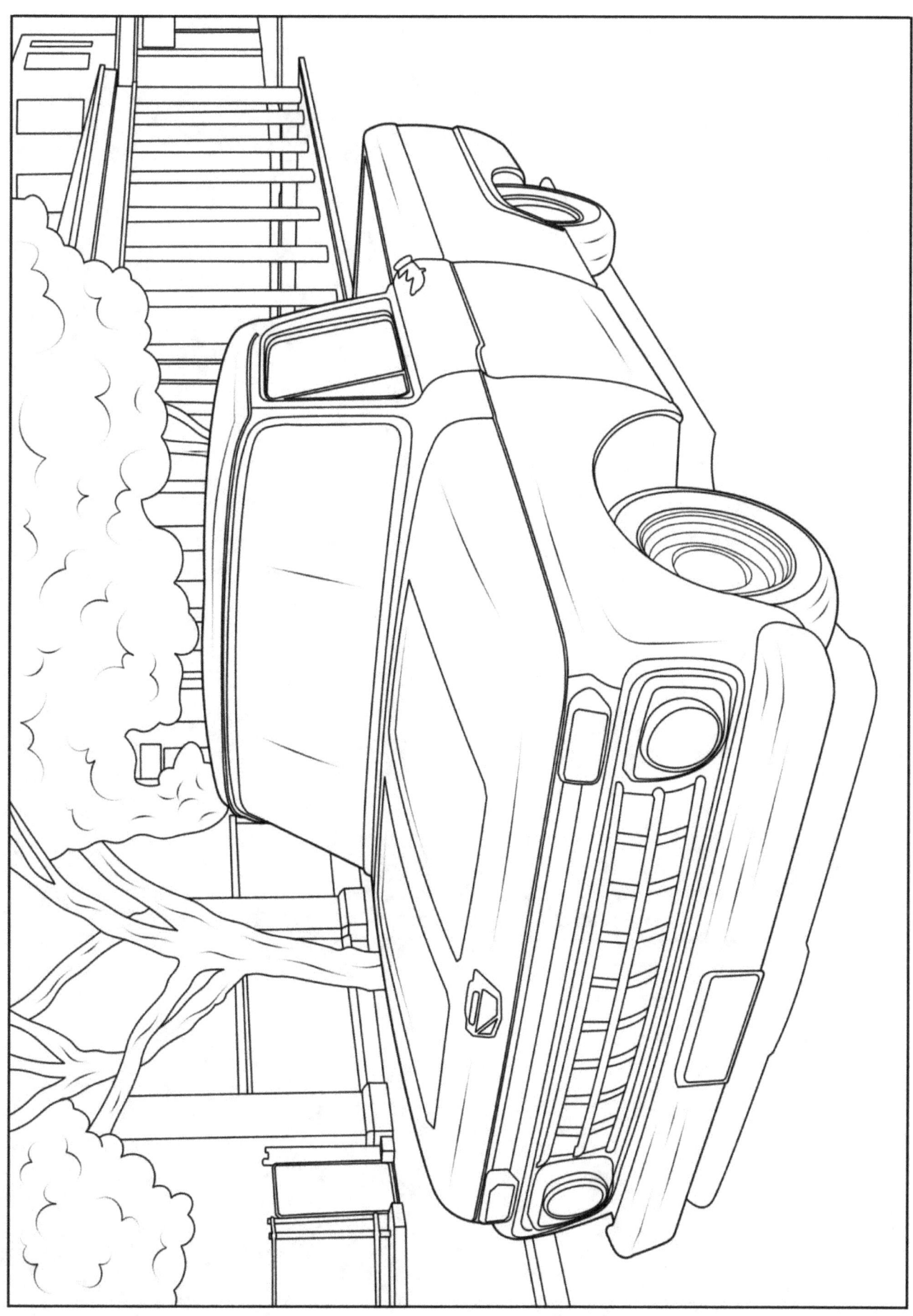

New Chevy style and power turned the tide and created a collectors' treasure.

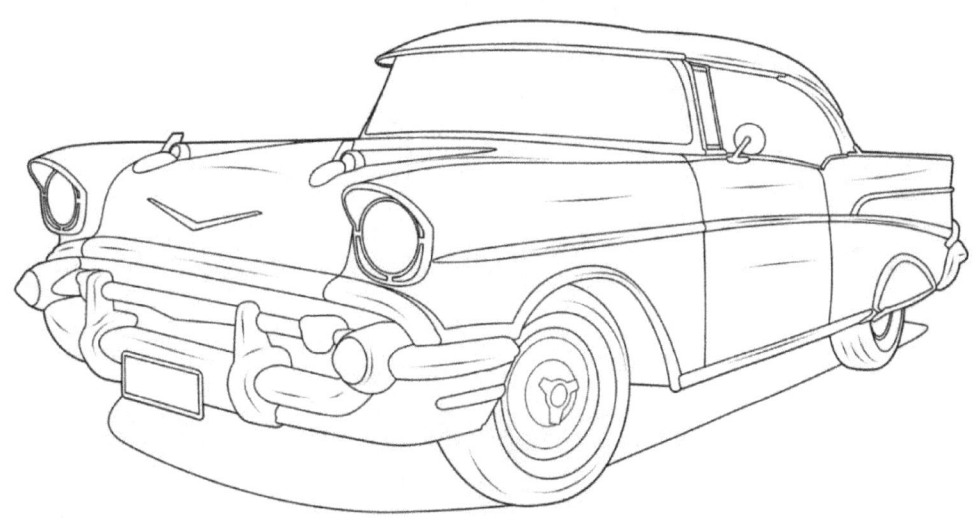

Chevrolet Bel Air (1949-1980)

No collection of American cars is fully complete without the ultra-iconic 1957 Chevy Bel Air. This car absolutely epitomizes 1950s car culture.

In the mid-'50s competition between Ford and Chevrolet for supremacy was more intense than ever. Ford had experienced great success with its Crestliner, Thunderbird and Customline models, to name but a few. What turned the tide was the "Tri-Five" Chevrolet line of models in 1955, 1956 & 1957 – particularly the 150, 210, Nomad and Bel Air models. They swung Chevrolet's market position significantly upward. Perhaps one of the most influential features of the Tri-Five was the newly developed 265 cubic-inch, small-block V8 with high compression and overhead valve engine. This was to be the beating heart of many other Chevys for several more decades.

The mid-'50s were watershed years for Chevrolet. It had invested heavily to retool its factory and make its Bel Air look more like a Cadillac. The '57 model received huge tailfins, a "twin rocket" hood design, three color paint options and seven different V8 engine choices. With this exciting recipe of style plus a power plant to match, the '57 Chevy managed to outsell its Ford rivals for the first time in years. It remains one of the most sought-after collectors' cars from any manufacturer.

Model illustrated:	1957 Chevrolet Bel Air Hardtop Sport Coupé with 265 cu.i. engine
Power:	170 hp
Engine:	265 cu.i. (4,343 cc) V8 gasoline with RWD
Weight:	3,273 lbs / 1,485 kg
0-60:	10.3 seconds (approx.)
Top Speed:	96 mph
Numbers Produced:	1,500,000 (approx. for the '57 model)

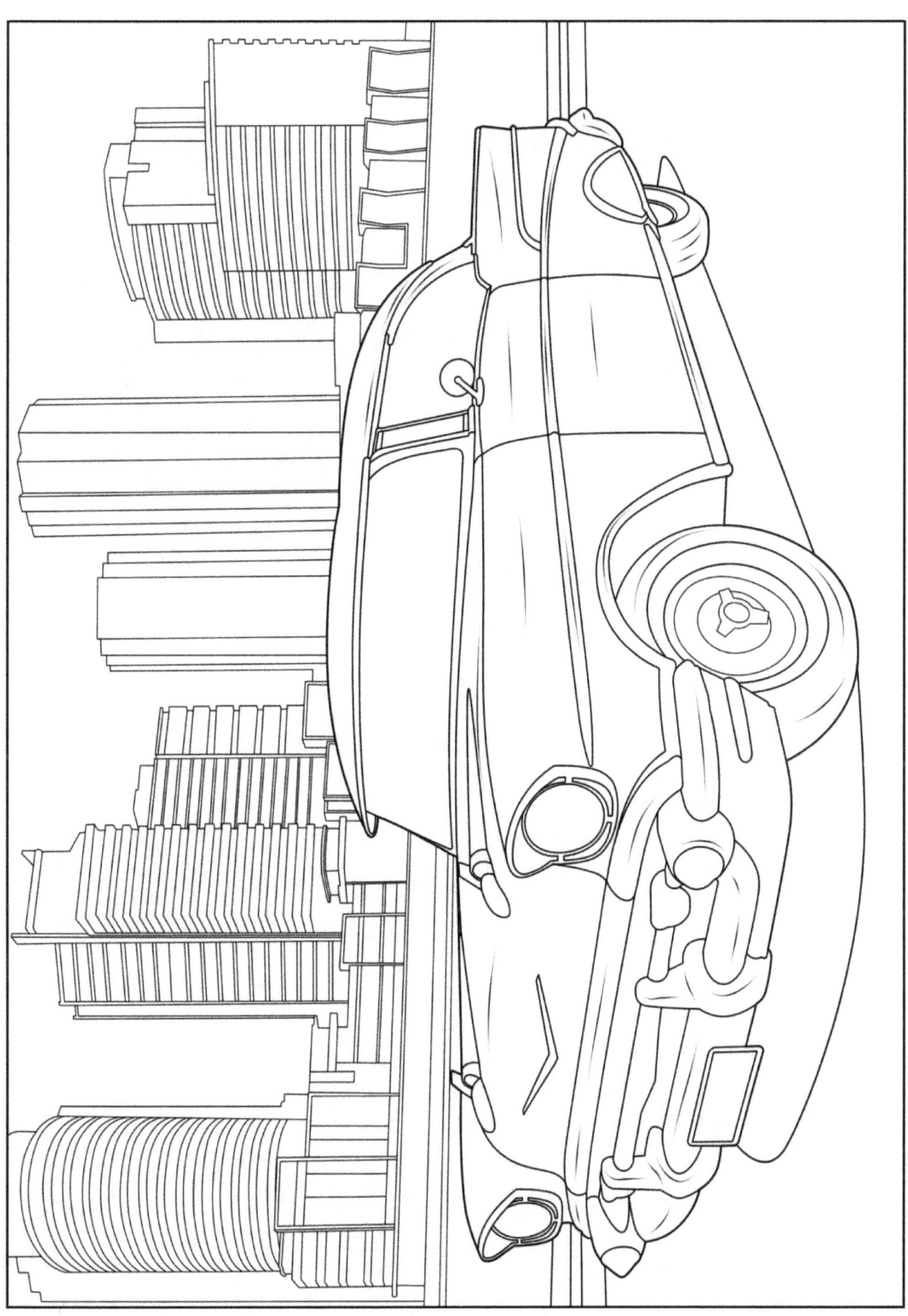

Blast off! How the very new Olds invented the American muscle car

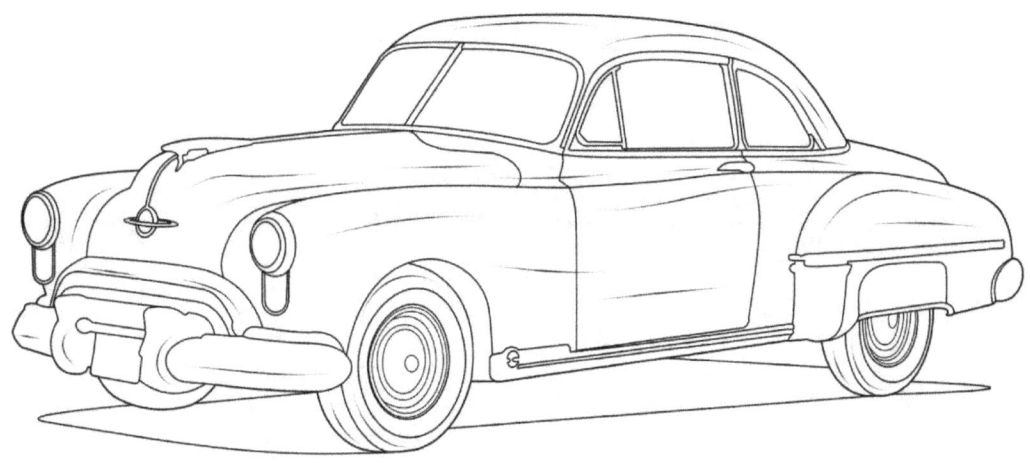

Oldsmobile Rocket 88 (1949–1999)

So, what was the first ever muscle car? This age-old discussion is unlikely to ever be fully concluded. But on one side of this argument many car historians believe the accolade deservedly belongs to the Oldsmobile Rocket 88. Although it wasn't realized at the time, the Olds 88 had all the prerequisites appropriate to a muscle car: a big V8, great performance, smooth flowing lines, and a relatively lightweight body.

This car was destined for great things. Its formula was copied repeatedly for many years to come. Such was the 88's success, that it rocketed Oldsmobile's image from "conservative" to "dynamic" and "high performance". The Olds soon became "the one to beat" and by the early '50s had earned the title "King of NASCAR".

The Olds 88 stood the test of time. Beloved through half a century and 10 different generations, it inspired the 1950s slogan "Make a Date with a Rocket 88". The song "Rocket 88" is often considered to be the first rock 'n' roll record, kicking off a whole new genre of music.

Production ceased in 1999 and the 88 was replaced with the Aurora model in 2001. The Olds 88 was one of the most impactful cars of its generation and gave birth to one of the most exciting and highly regarded vehicular sectors – the American muscle car.

Model illustrated:	1949 Oldsmobile Rocket 88
Power:	135 hp
Engine:	303 cui. (4,965cc) V8 gasoline with RWD
Weight:	3,580 lbs / 1,624 kg
0-60:	13 seconds (approx.)
Top Speed:	97 mph
Numbers Produced:	10,000,000 (approx. across all generations)

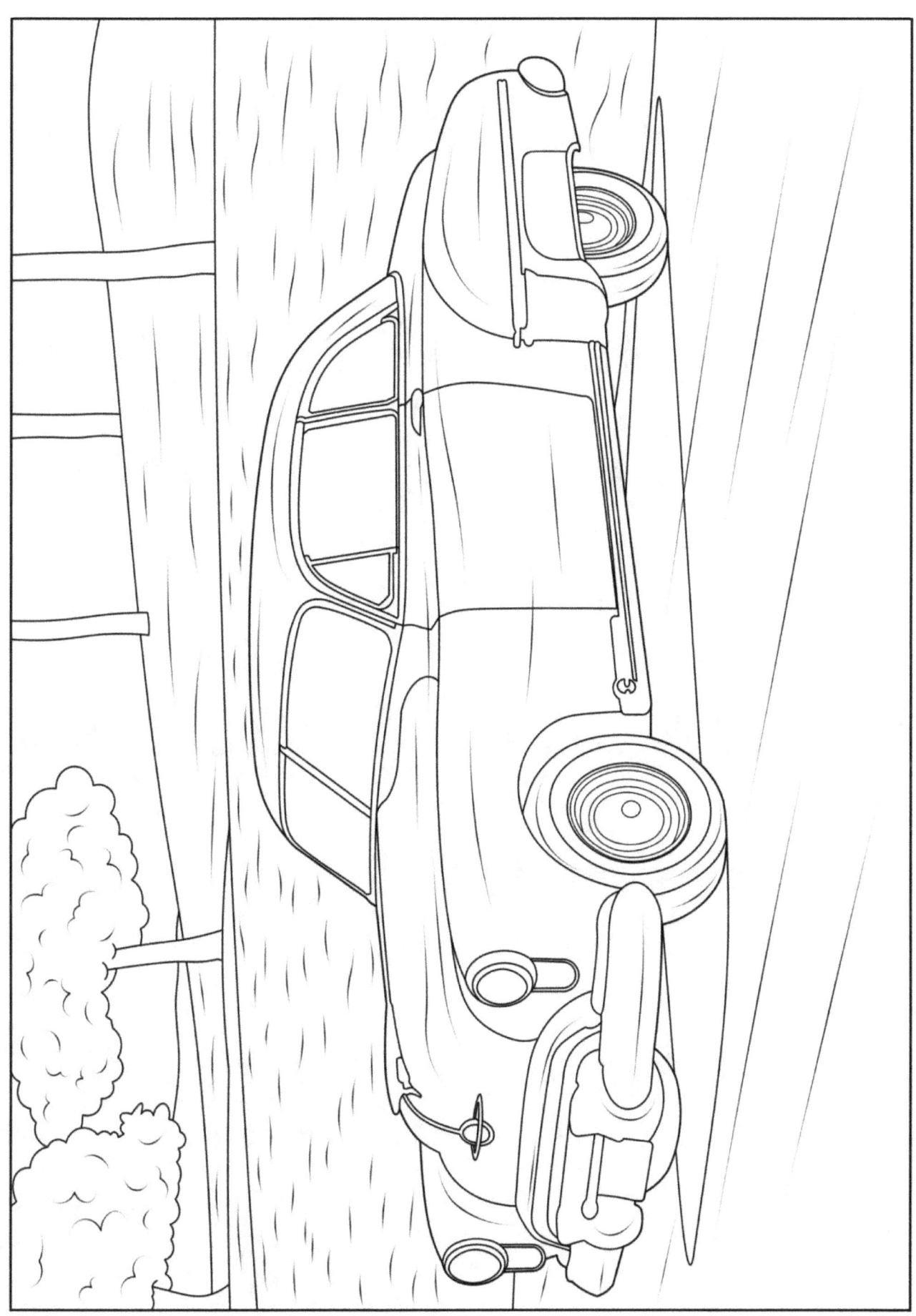

Cadillac's Eldorado redefined luxury cars and hit a 50-year seam of golden sales.

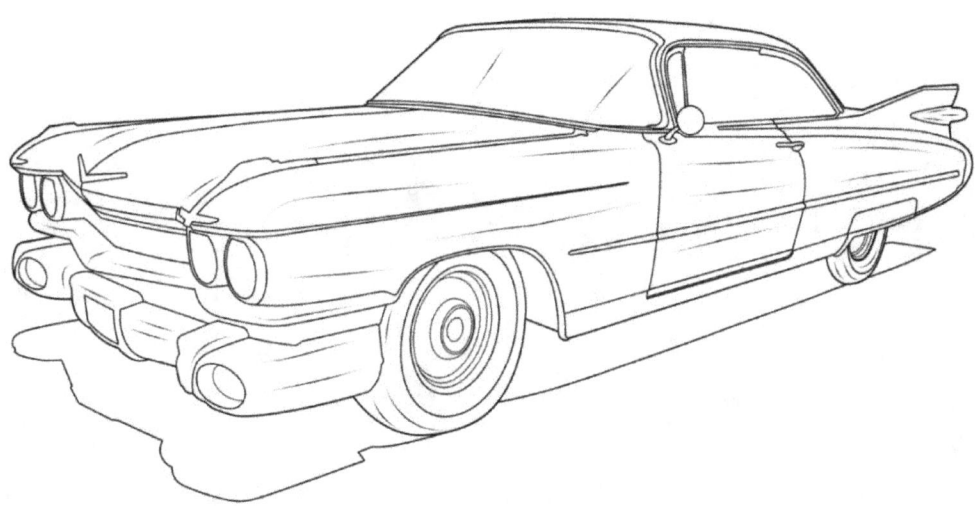

Cadillac Eldorado (1952-2002)

From what was initially an inhouse naming competition for an anniversary show car, the Eldorado was a success story for a model that sat near the top of the Cadillac model line-up for half a century. The name itself is a contraction of two Spanish words that translate to be 'The Golden One'. It also references the mythical 'Lost City of Gold' where the tribal chief, as an initiation ritual, covered himself in gold dust and then submerged himself into Lake Guatavita. Cadillac showrooms, with their Eldorado models, became places of untold sales success for the next 50 years.

With its 98-inch tailfins, the fourth-generation 1959 model took contemporary car styling to ridiculous new heights. The result was one of the most timeless and iconic American cars ever. With memories of economic hardship in the Great Depression of the 1930s finally fading after World War II, US consumers were now ready to spend their money on cars offering refinement and luxury. And if it was luxury they wanted, it was luxury that the Eldorado delivered – with a comfortable ride and technologically advanced features such as air suspension. The Eldorado spawned a new market segment of its own, brushing off stiff competition from Lincoln's Mark Series, Buick's Riviera and the Chrysler Imperial.

In 2002 the Eldorado celebrated its milestone golden anniversary as a car that pushed the boundaries of what was possible to their limits.

Model illustrated:	1959 2 Door Cadillac Eldorado Seville (Hardtop)
Power:	345 hp
Engine:	390 cui. (6,382 cc) naturally aspirated V8 gasoline with RWD
Weight:	5,060 lbs / 2,295 kg
0-60:	10.3 seconds (approx.)
Top Speed:	127 mph
Numbers Produced:	142,000 (approx. for the '59 model year incl. Seville and Biarritz models)

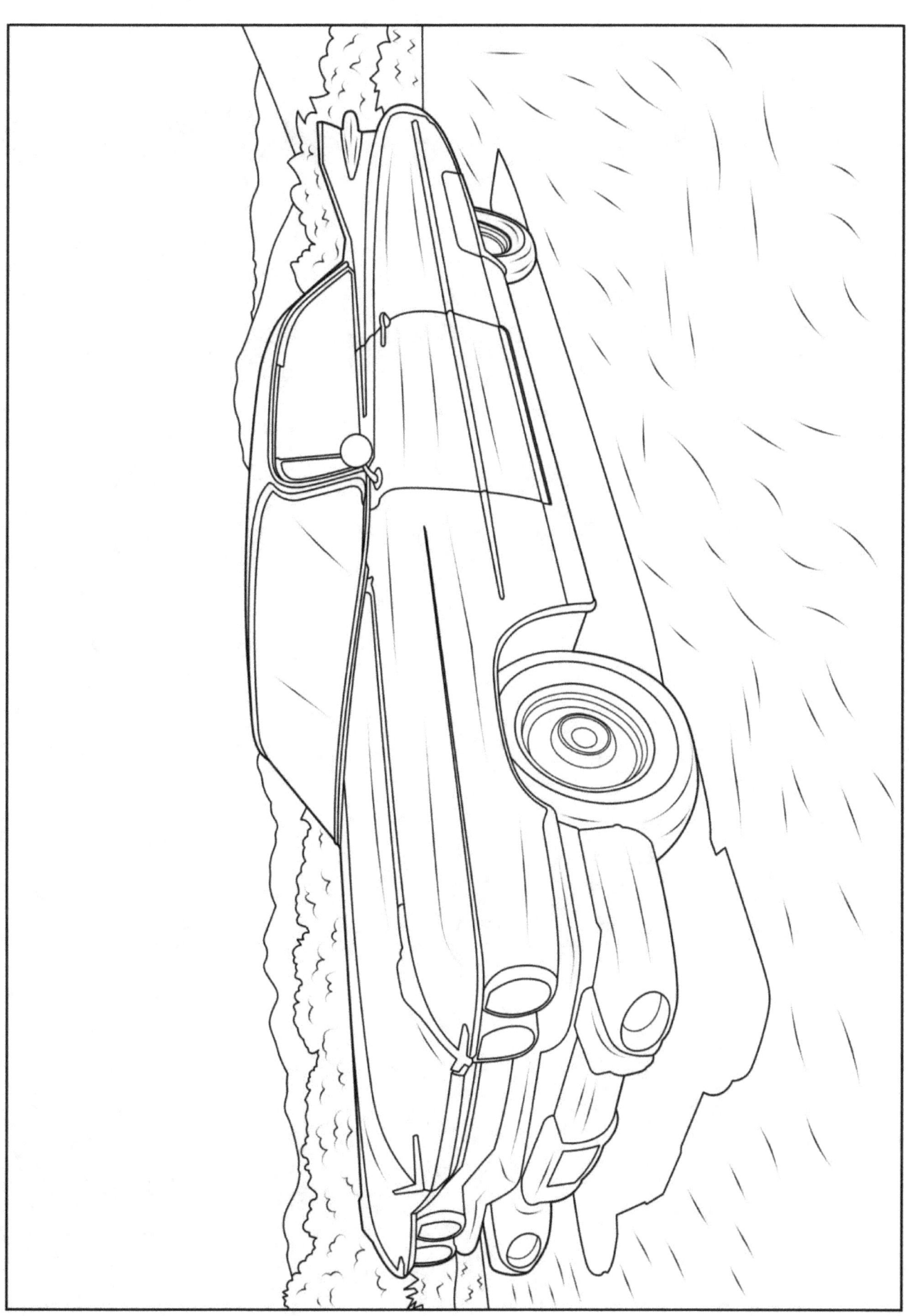

America's sports car –
The sting in its tail scored an instant hit.

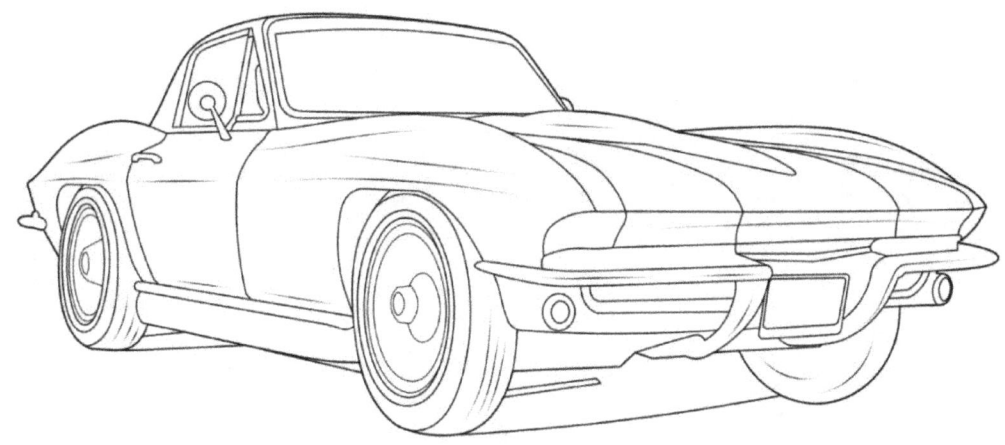

Chevrolet Corvette (1953-Present)

With a name derived from a small and nimble warship the Corvette (often shortened to "Vette") was always going to be destined for great things. Now in its eighth generation, the Vette has been Chevrolet's halo model for nearly seven decades.

The first Corvette rolled off the production line in 1953, became an instant hit, and very quickly earned the title of "America's Sports Car". Having starred in the hugely successful television show Route 66, the car soon became synonymous with freedom and adventure.

The first-generation Corvette enjoyed a decade of huge sales success while the Chevrolet Research & Development team poured significant resources into the next iteration of this GM halo car. So, the second and perhaps most gloriously styled Corvette model was created – the Corvette C2. With the introduction of the C2 came a new name – the "Stingray" or "Sting Ray", evoking an immediate connection to the venomous-tailed ocean fish. With its low, flat lines, closed headlights, split rear window, muscular fenders and long back the car looked ready to sting any competition on the road. The Stingray's lines reflected the futuristic, angular "Googie" design language popular in the mid 20th century.

But on the road, the Stingray established itself as a world-class sports car and has inspired Chevrolet sports cars for decades since.

Model illustrated: 1963 Chevrolet Corvette Stingray 2 Door Coupe
Power: 300 hp
Engine: 327 cu.i. (5,354 cc) naturally aspirated V8 gasoline with RWD
Weight: 3,362 lbs / 1,525 kg
0-60:   6 seconds
Top Speed: 130 mph
Numbers Produced: 117,966 (for C2 model)

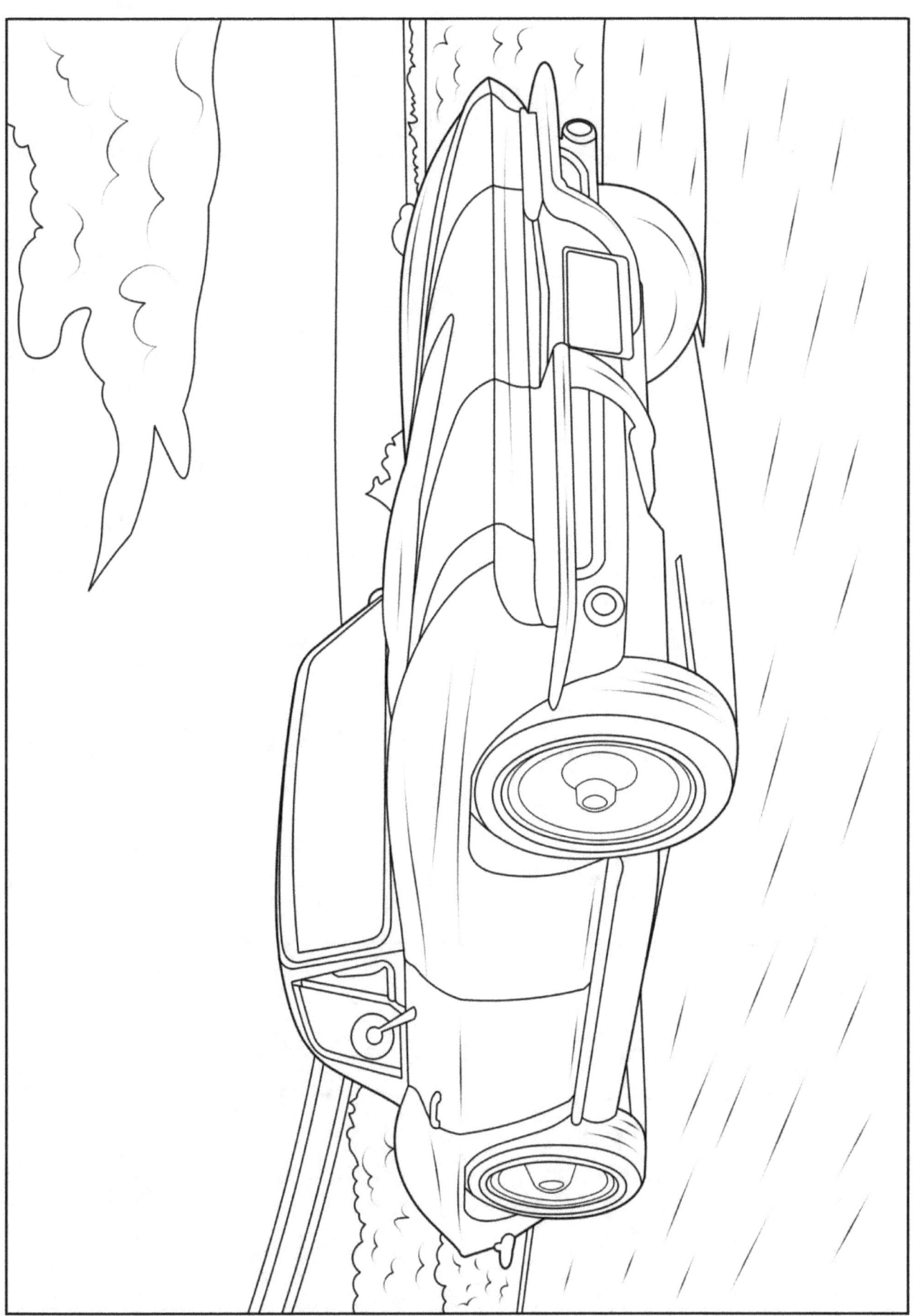

Twilight falls on America's love affair with big sedans.

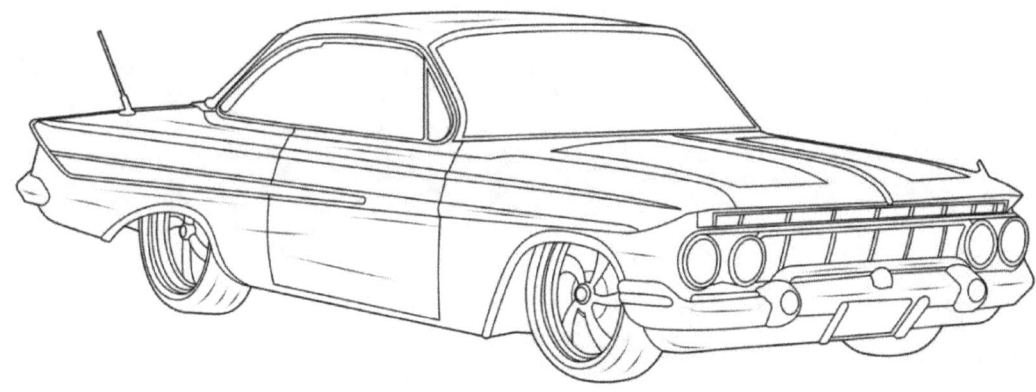

Chevrolet Impala (1957-1985, 1994-1996, 1999-Present)

When first introduced in 1958, the Chevy Impala offered Americans a comfortable, yet affordable full-size car. And ever since, across its various body styles the Impala has remained the essence of the American car industry. Despite its rather bumpy ride over the years, including a production hiatus from the mid '80s to the mid '90s, the Impala offered Americans an excellent and successful automotive recipe spanning generations.

The Impala's graceful lines seem to personify the African antelope from which it took its name. And with styling cues from the sporty Chevy Corvette, it quickly became known as the "Corvette Impala" across the motoring press. In an era when the auto industry was booming, and road travel was up by over 50% on American roads, the Impala was quick to fill the demand for performance, comfort and style. It offered a good quality product for consumers' hard-earned dollars.

Having made it through 10 generations of a hugely successful production lifecycle, demand for full-size sedans cars like the Impala has slowly dwindled with the increasing popularity of the SUV and Crossover markets. And so, the Impala model has been laid to rest while retaining a significant place in the hearts of so many Americans.

Model illustrated: Third-generation 1961 Impala "Bubble Top" Sport Coupe
Power: 135 hp
Engine: 235.5 cu.i. (3,859 cc) naturally aspirated six-cylinder gasoline with RWD
Weight: 3,485 lbs / 1,581 kg
0-60:   14.5 seconds
Top Speed: 93 mph
Numbers Produced: 16,500,000+ (approx. across all 10 generations)

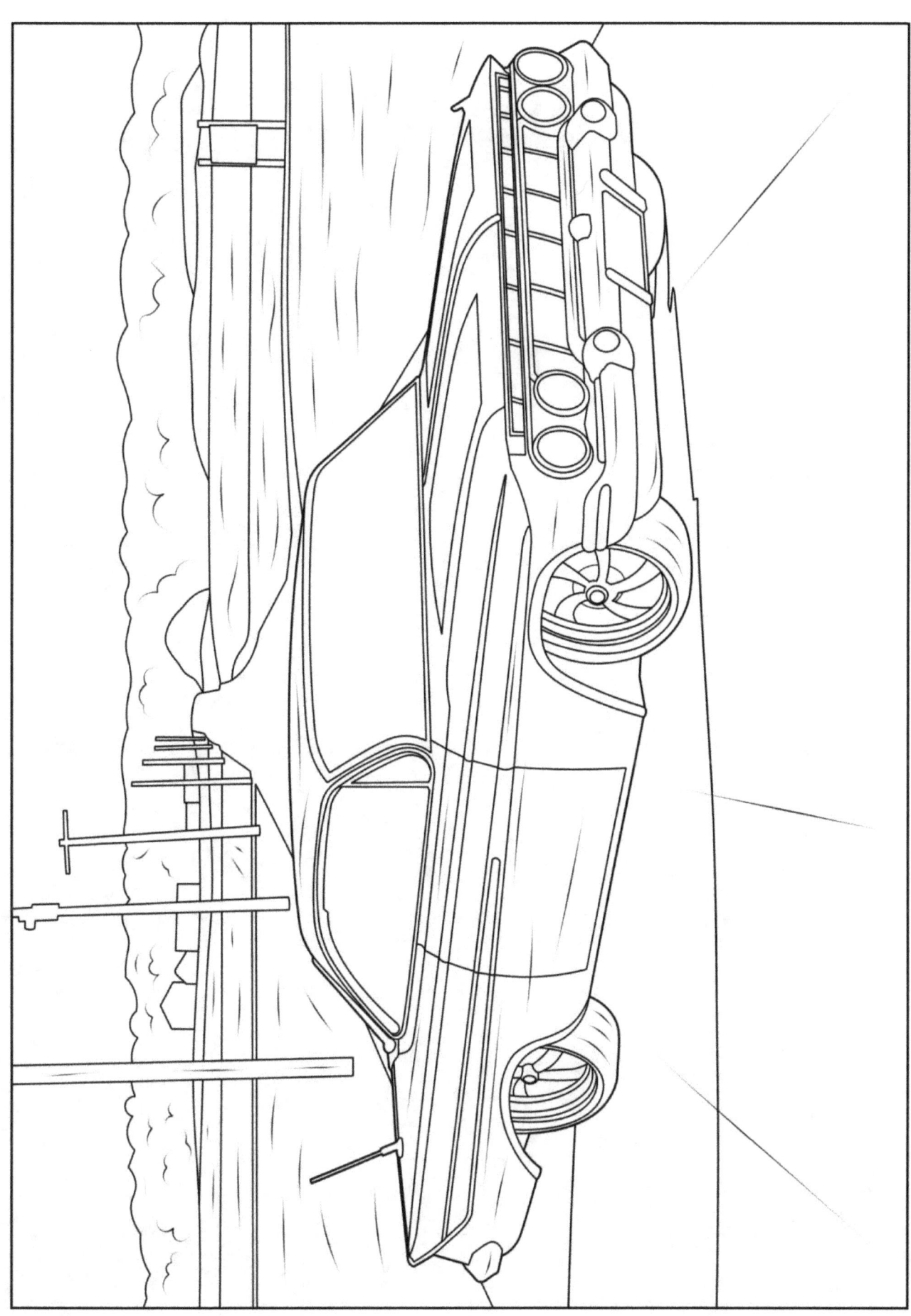

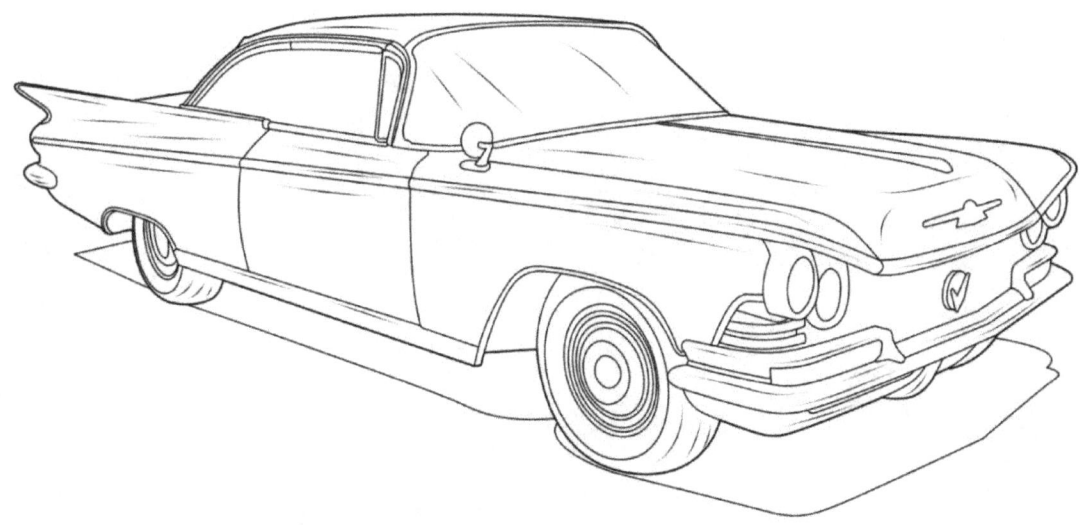

Buick Electra (1959-1990)

The Electra was Buick's full-size luxury offering and successfully spanned six generations from its launch in 1959 through to 1990.

Named after the spectacularly wealthy Texas-born sculptor and heiress Electra Waggoner Biggs, the Electra was built to succeed the immensely popular Buick Super and Buick Roadmaster. Both the Electra and the Electra 225 shared the GM C-body platform with the Oldsmobile 98 and mid-level Cadillacs of the era. The "225" nameplate was a nod to its overall length of just over 225 inches (18 ¾ feet) which was nearly five inches longer than the standard Electra model, helping earn its street name of "deuce and a quarter".

Various body styles were available across its history including a coupé, convertible, sedan, and station wagon. The Electra was rear-wheel driven for its first five generations. Power came mainly in the form of Buick "Nailhead" V8s. A V6 engine was introduced for the fifth-generation model, delivering power to the rear wheels. It wasn't until the sixth-generation, from 1984 through 1990, that a new direction of Electra came, down-sized and re-designed, with front-wheel drive. Sadly, the sixth generation was the last of the very successful Electra. Its power, style and grace had made an impact on the American public.

Model illustrated:	1959 Buick Electra 225 Coupé
Power:	325 hp
Engine:	401 cu.i. (6,572 cc) n/a 'Nailhead' V8 gasoline with RWD
Weight:	4,810 lbs / 2,180 kg
0-60:	9.5 seconds
Top Speed:	124 mph
Numbers Produced:	11,216 (Electra 2-Door Hardtop models in 1959)

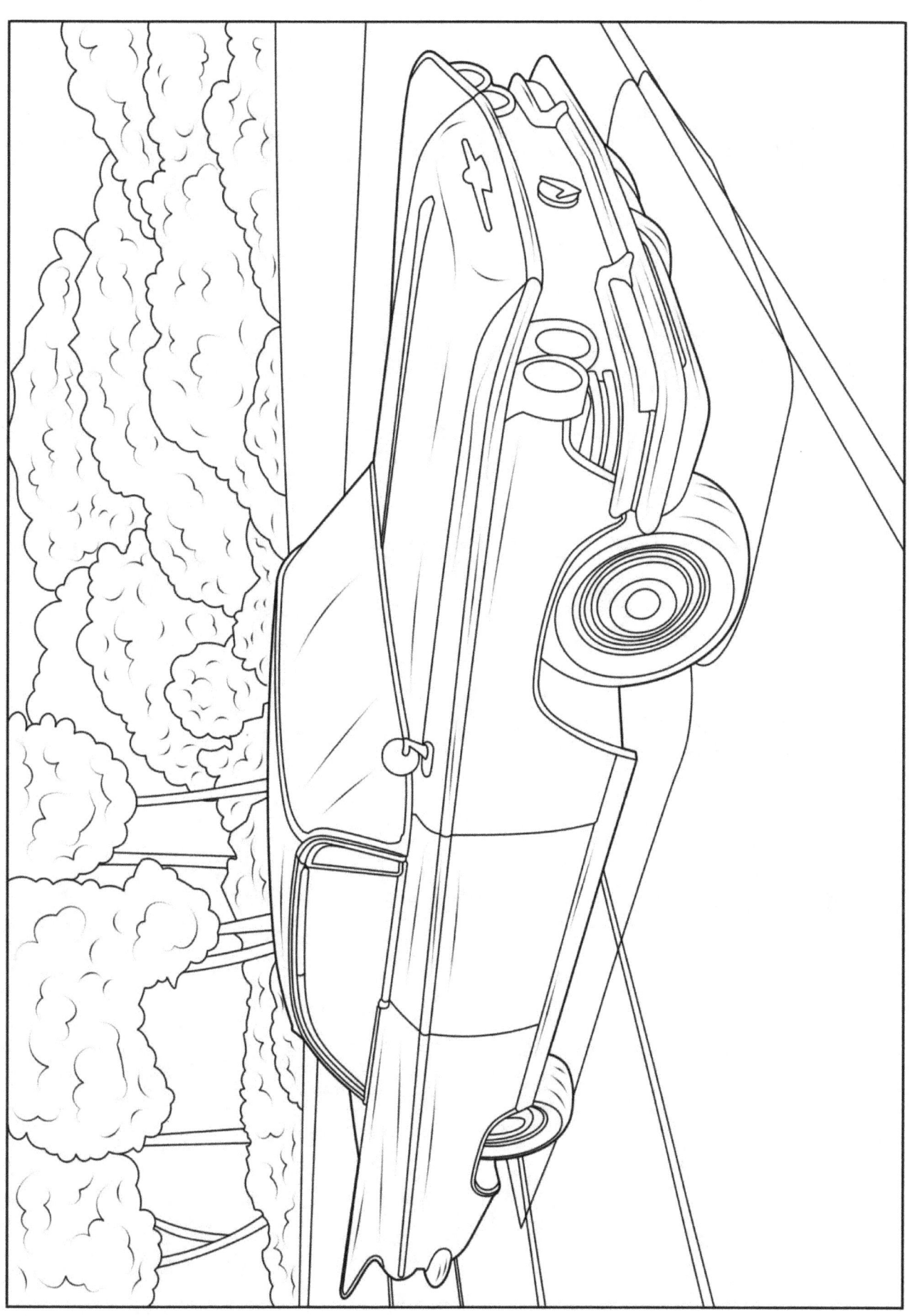

Opportunity strikes and delivers a transatlantic car-making partnership.

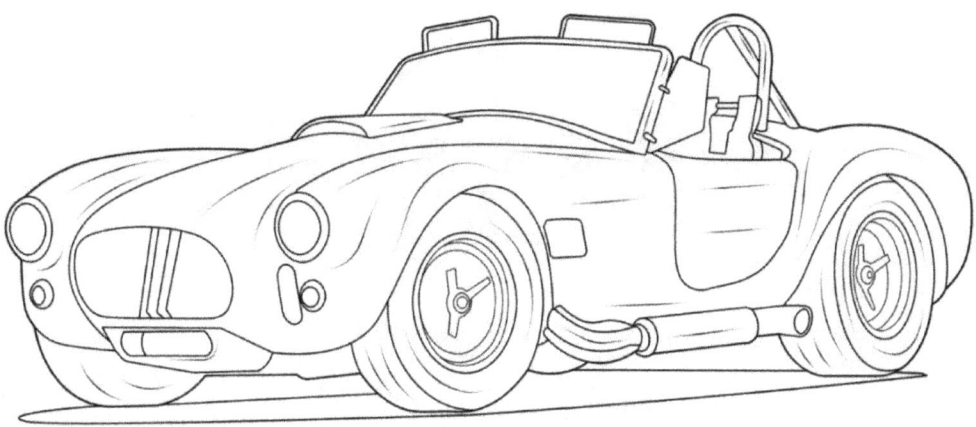

Shelby Cobra (1962-1967)

With the Shelby Cobra we probably have one of the great Anglo-American engineering partnerships. In 1962 American racing driver/car designer Carroll Shelby learned that AC Cars could no longer continue to make its two-seater roadster model, the AC Ace, at Thames Ditton in Surrey, England. AC's engine supplier, Bristol, was ceasing production of its straight-six engine, which had been around since before WWII. Quick to see the opportunity, Shelby bought a number of engineless car bodies across to his Venice Beach shop in California, where he had Ford V8 engines ready to install.

Before crossing the Atlantic, Shelby's AC Cobra chassis needed many modifications to cope with the increased V8 power going under their hoods. Much of the front end of the car was re-worked, the steering was modified, a stronger rear differential was designed for the increased power and a new steering system was created. Once AC Cars had tested the blend and declared itself happy with the result, the test engines and transmissions were removed and the bodies were air-freighted to the eager Shelby in L.A. In went Shelby's 260 cu.i. V8 and, within eight hours, each new car was ready for testing.

Over time the Shelby Cobra had several powertrains under the hood, ranging from the very first 260 cu.i. V8 through to a big block 390 and, ultimately, the 427 cu.i. "FE" engine of the Mark III variant.

Nevertheless, the Shelby Cobra was a commercial failure – but its limited numbers make original examples extremely desirable and incredibly expensive in today's market.

Model illustrated:	1966 Shelby Cobra 427
Power:	410 hp
Engine:	425.98 cu.i. (6,997 cc) n/a big block V8 gasoline with RWD
Weight:	2,529 lbs / 1,147 kg
0-60:	4.5 seconds
Top Speed:	165 mph
Numbers Produced:	348 (from 1965-1967)

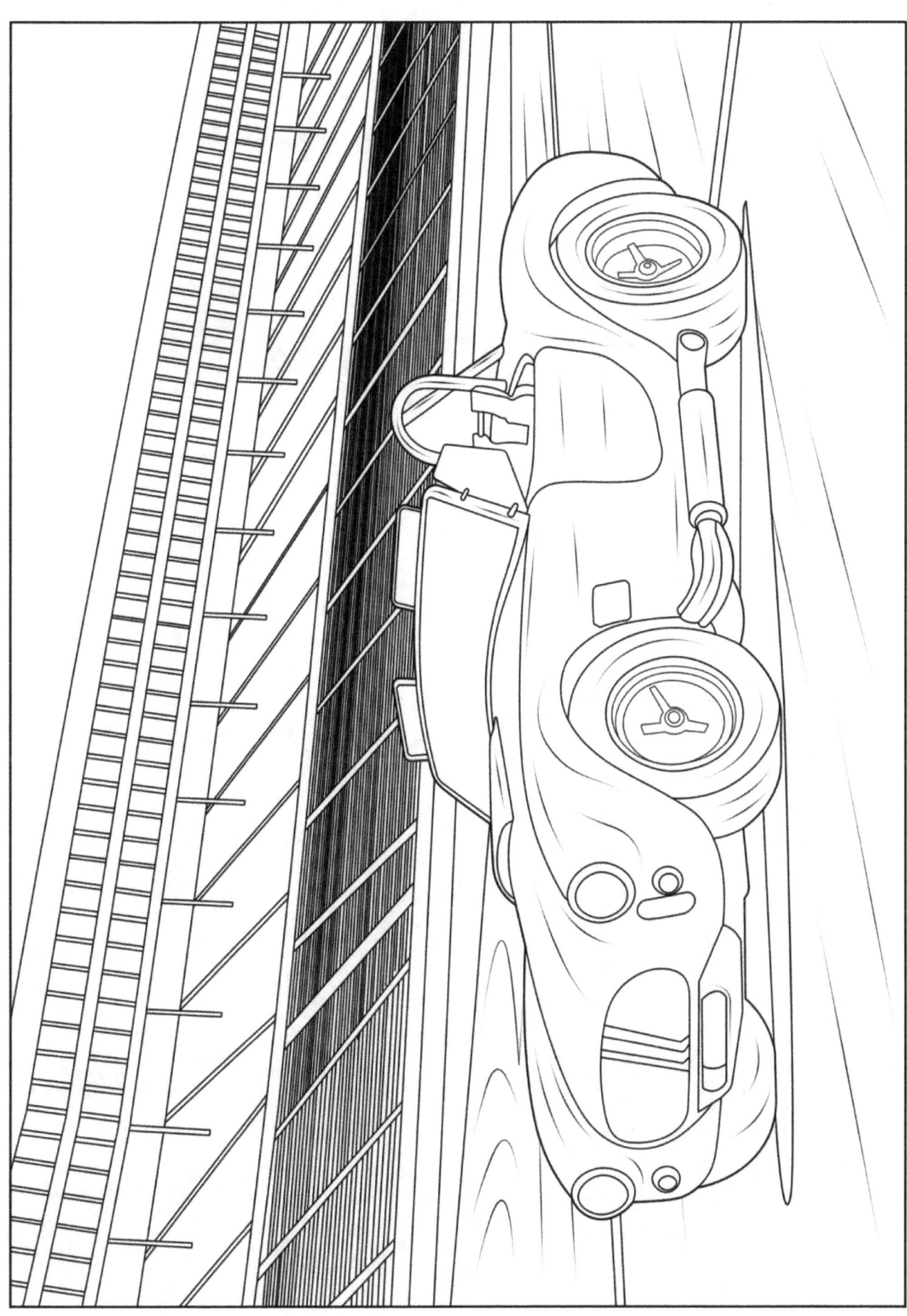

From rag trade to riches with the Big Apple's iconic yellow cab.

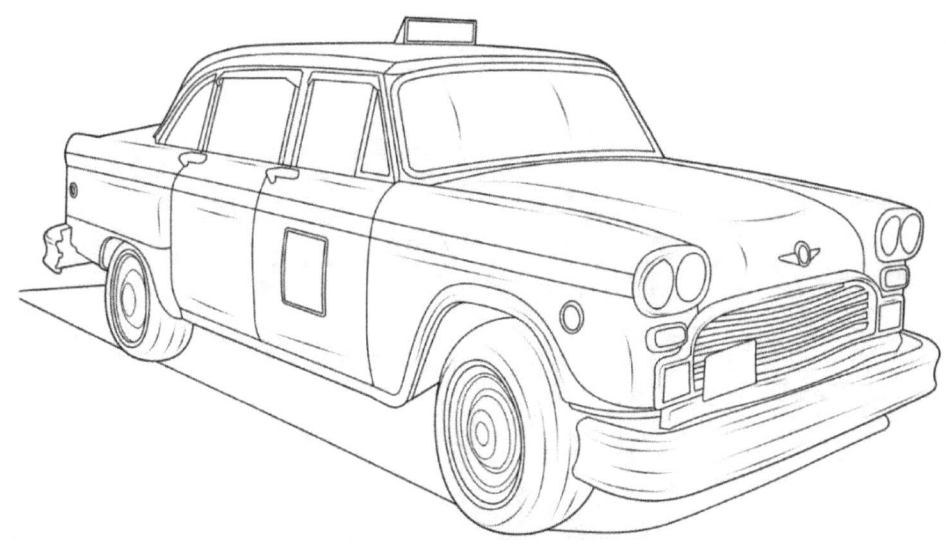

Checker A11 Taxi (1963-1982)

With a history dating back nearly 100 years, the Checker Motors Corporation created a car that, at some point along the way, most Americans and many others from across the globe will have ridden in at least once in their lifetime.

Russian-Jewish tailor Morris Markin, who emigrated to the USA in 1913, had established a successful ready-to-wear suits business in Chicago. Then fellow immigrant Ade Lomberg asked Markin to loan him money for his business with Commonwealth Motors, who manufactured bodies for luxury automobiles and purpose-built taxi cabs. When both Commonwealth Motors and Lomberg failed within a year, Markin assumed control. The Checker Taxi company of Chicago was born.

Perhaps the most successful car in its history was the Checker Model A11 which remained mostly unchanged over a 20-year production cycle. Most A11s ran a 230 cu.i. Chevrolet inline 6-cylinder engine with a 283 or 327 V8 being available as an option. New York fully adopted the Checker as its taxi vehicle of choice and it gradually became one of the most instantly recognizable vehicles in the world — a rolling, anachronistic symbol of NYC.

Model illustrated:	1967 Checker A11 Taxi
Power:	140 hp
Engine:	230 cu.i. (3,768 cc) n/a six-cylinder gasoline with RWD
Weight:	3,390 lbs / 1,620 kg
0-60:	14 seconds
Top Speed:	90 mph
Numbers Produced:	100,000 (approx.)

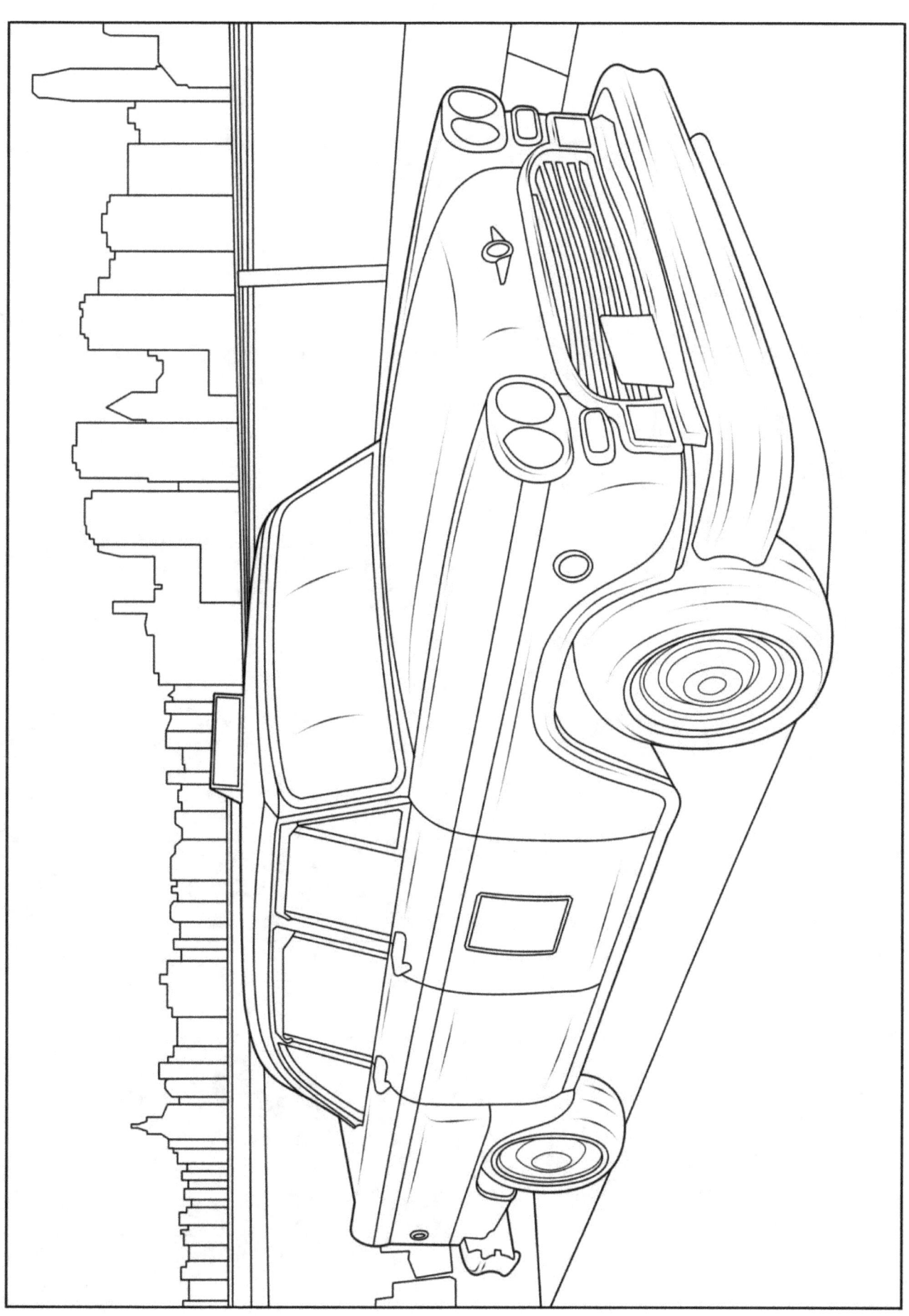

Once a truck, now an icon... it was the grandfather of modern SUVs.

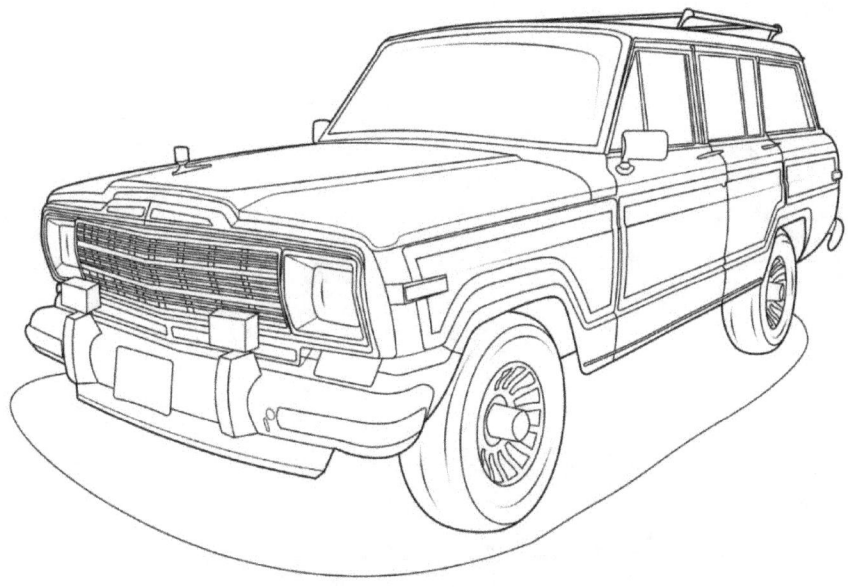

Jeep Grand Wagoneer (1963–1991)

A forebearer of today's modern SUVs, the Jeep Grand Wagoneer was first introduced in 1963 to succeed the utilitarian Willys Jeep Station Wagon, ending its 17-year production run. The Wagoneer was originally based on the chassis of a pickup truck, but offered offer class-leading comfort with very respectable off-road capability in a sophisticated station wagon body. Luxuries elevated the Wagoneer from truck to classy SUV – including independent front suspension, automatic transmission, a factory installed radio system and, most importantly, air conditioning.

Despite being produced for 29 years, the Grand Wagoneer was manufactured by three different parent companies. First Kaiser, who originally needed to replace the ageing Willys Jeep Station Wagon. Then in the early 1970s AMC, who began refining and upgrading the whole driving experience – they reduced engine noise, vibration, and harshness to keep the Wagoneer at the forefront of American car buyers' taste. But it wasn't until Chrysler bought out AMC in 1987 that the "best in breed" and most coveted Wagoneers were produced. The most easily recognizable models featured an upgraded vinyl-wood side panel, refreshed exterior colors, improved interior finishes and modernized styling.

Despite abysmal combined fuel economy (11 mpg!) the Wagoneer maintained strong brand loyalty through the 1960s, '70s and '80s, becoming the longest-running vehicle on the same platform with over 100,000 cars sold.

Model illustrated:	1987 Jeep Grand Wagoneer
Power:	245 hp
Engine:	360 cu.i. (5,896 cc) n/a V8 gasoline with RWD or AWD (All-Wheel Drive)
Weight:	4,760 lbs / 2,159 kg
0-60:	11.9 seconds
Top Speed:	75 mph
Numbers Produced:	101,637 (Grand Wagoneer models)

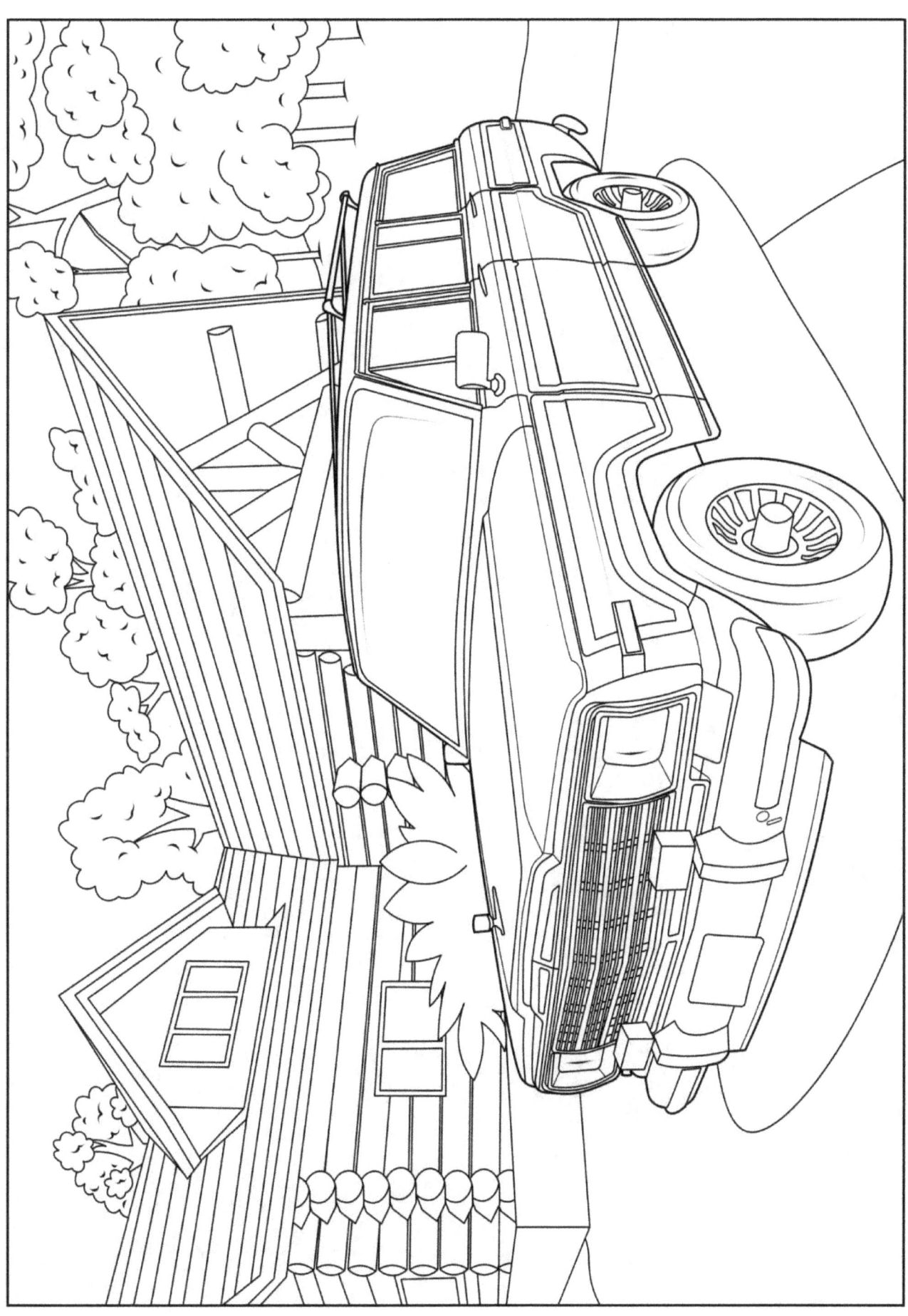

Legendary Italian designer declared his love for "one of the most beautiful American cars ever".

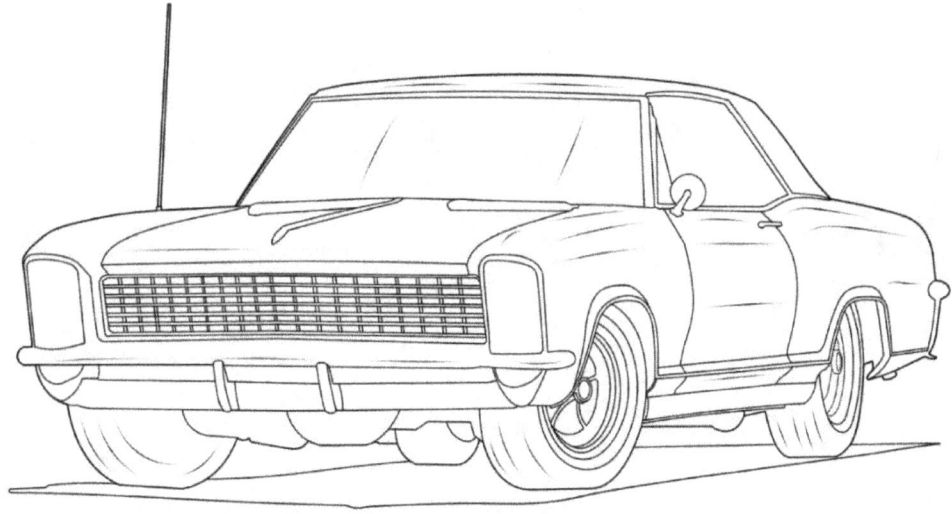

Buick Riviera (1963–1999)

Legendary Italian car designer Sergio Pininfarina, whose studio is said to have designed more beautiful cars than any other, declared the Buick Riviera "one of the most beautiful American cars ever produced". Inspired by the allure and affluence of the French Riviera, that was exactly what General Motors' Buick brand had in mind for its first entry into the luxury car market. The Riviera intended to compete with the truly impressive Ford Thunderbird, (which had been introduced as a two-seater convertible, then upscaled to a four-passenger model). The Riviera quickly followed suit with its distinctive body shell and elegant "Coke Bottle" styling, and was an instant sales success.

Having lasted eight generations and an almost uninterrupted production lifespan (it had a brief hiatus in 1994) the Riviera has proven itself to be America's preeminent personal luxury car. The last 200 Rivieras to roll off the production line were finished in a special silver paint and trim and given the "Silver Arrow" name in homage to the original Silver Arrow cars which Bill Mitchell, the Riviera's first designer, had built off Riviera bodies.

Since production ceased in 1999, two concept Riviera models have been shown at the Shanghai Motor Show – in 2007 and 2013. Both concept models featured radical gullwing-style doors and avant garde styling. Sadly, neither concept made it into full production and the Riviera moniker remains dormant, for now.

Model illustrated:	1965 Buick Riviera Gran Sport 2 Door Hardtop
Power:	325 hp
Engine:	425 cu.i. (6,970 cc) naturally aspirated "Nailhead" V8 gasoline with RWD
Weight:	4,036 lbs / 1,831 kg
0-60:	7.9 seconds
Top Speed:	124 mph
Numbers Produced:	1,127,261 (across all generations)

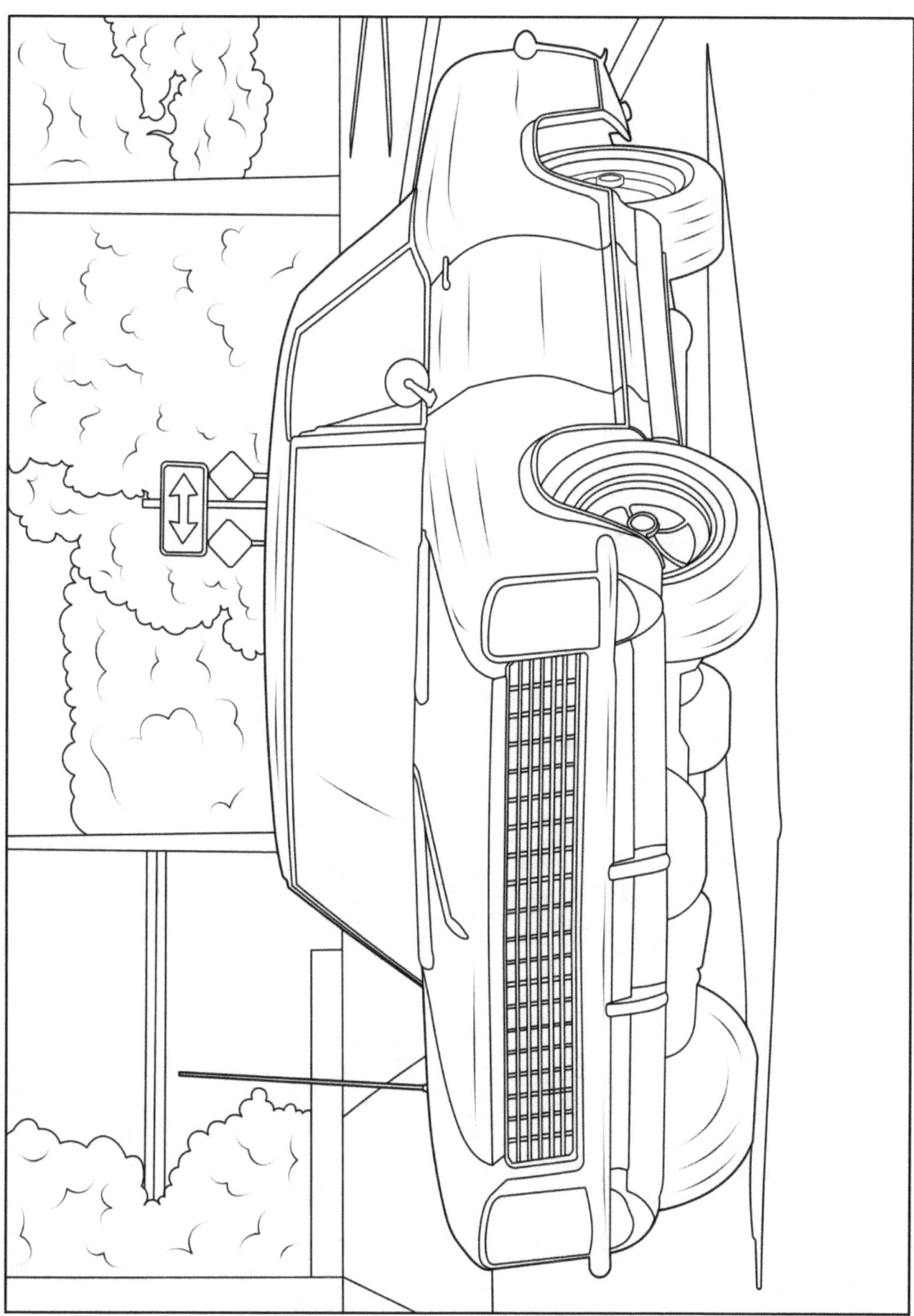

Revenge on wheels! How Mr. Ford found satisfaction for failed Ferrari takeover.

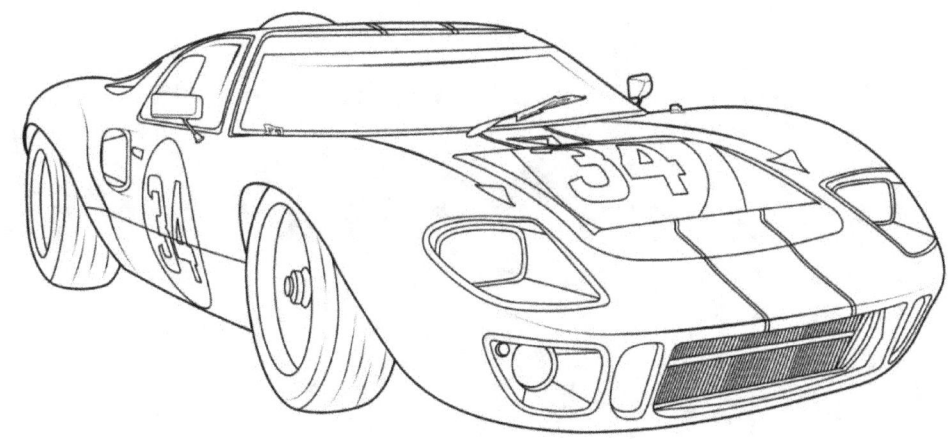

Ford GT40 (1964-1969)

In the 1960s Ford took on Ferrari and beat it at its own game with its legendary GT40 (the "40" referenced the car's height in inches). The GT40 was born of Henry Ford II's rage when Ferrari pulled out of his takeover attempt at the last minute. By the late '60s the GT40 wasn't just beating Ferrari, it was totally humiliating the great Italian racing team.

Henry Ford II had spent millions of dollars to audit Ferrari assets and prepare the legal process for his takeover of the iconic European car makers. Then Enzo Ferrari pulled out of the deal. In furious retaliation, Henry Ford II ordered a vendetta by his racing division. They had to build a car that would beat Ferrari on the world endurance racing circuit – at any cost.

A Lola Mk6 was agreed on for the Ferrari-beating car's chassis. It was to be the basis of development by a carefully selected Ford Racing Division team. And with the GT40 the team showed just what American automotive masterminds were capable of achieving when they set their minds to it. In 1966 all their hard work paid off with a crushing 1-2-3 victory in the Le Mans 24-Hour Race. It was just the first of four years dominating the iconic Le Mans racing series. The GT40 well and truly earned its place, reaching the pinnacle of American automotive engineering.

Model illustrated:	1968 Ford GT40 "P" Mk1 ("P" = production)
Power:	335 hp
Engine:	289 cu.i. (4,736 cc) naturally aspirated V8 gasoline with RWD
Weight:	2,205 lbs / 1,000 kg
0-60:	5.3 seconds
Top Speed:	164 mph
Numbers Produced:	124 (1964-1969 – Mk1, Mk2, Mk3 & Mk4)

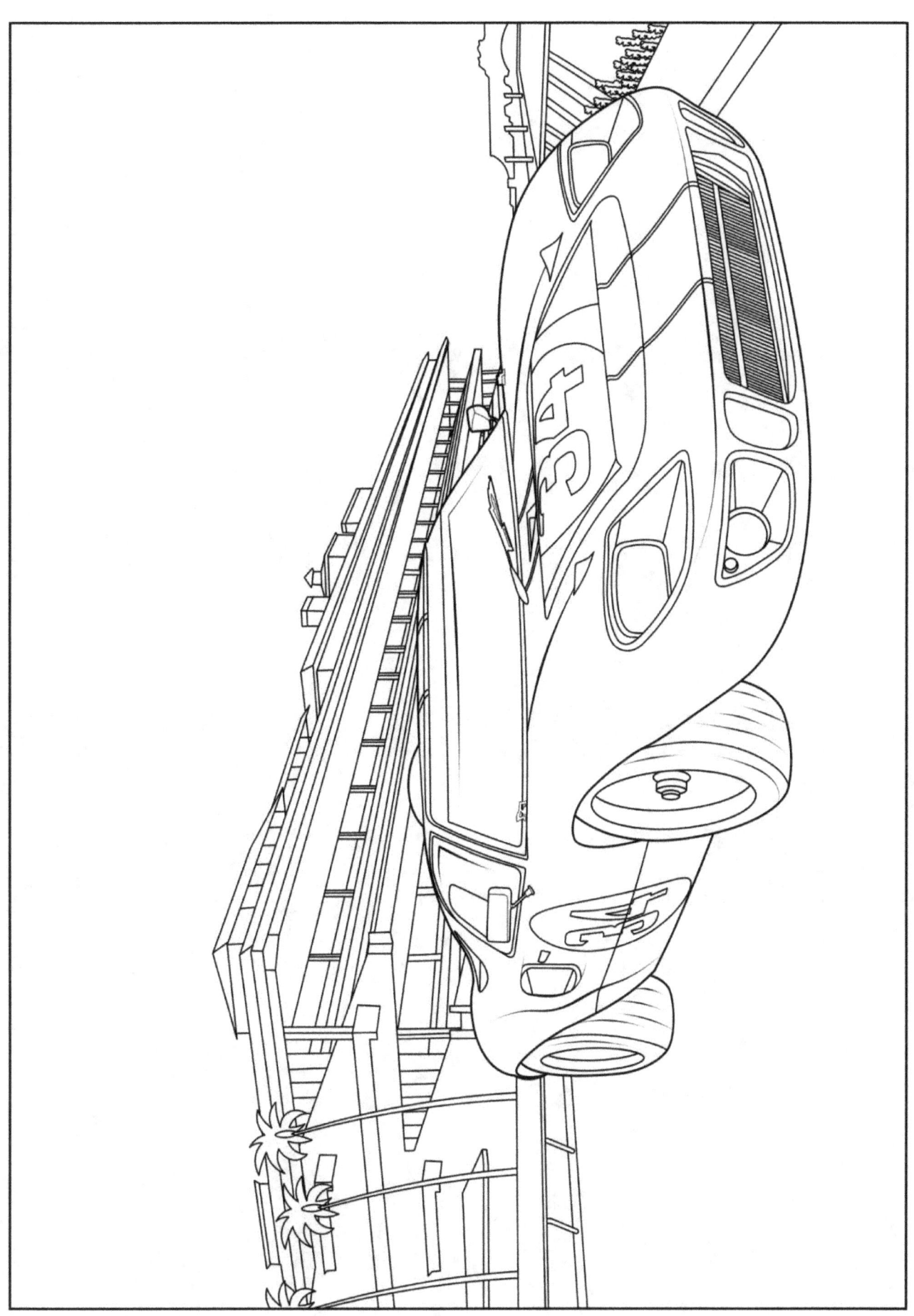

Automotive wolf in sheep's clothing sparked a power-car revolution.

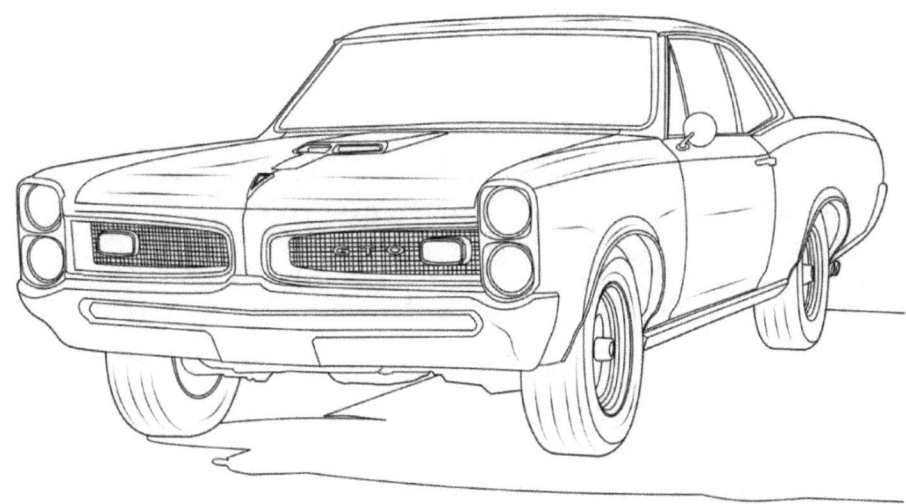

Pontiac GTO (1964-1974, 2004-2006)

No list of America's most iconic cars is fully complete without the inclusion of this wolf in sheep's clothing – the sleek, innocent-looking Pontiac GTO, one of the first of the muscle car revolutionaries.

In the mid 1950s, Pontiac was in desperate need to re-invigorate itself and appeal to a more youthful audience. So, they called in the former GM vice-president, Semon "Bunkie" Knudsen. Knudsen brought together a team of rather rebellious, extremely creative engineers with huge ambitions. The team included the likes of John DeLorean, Bill Collins, and Russ Gee, all at the top of their game at that time. The result was a car that not only launched an entirely new market, but one that started an automotive revolution.

It was commonplace at the time for no engines over 330 cubic inches to be allowed into mid-size GM vehicles. This didn't stop Knudsen's team of rebels shoehorning a 389 cubic-inch engine into the upcoming second-generation Pontiac Tempest. This subterfuge was made easier by the fact that both engines had similar fitments and dimensions despite their difference in power. The beefier engine was, in fact, the powerplant for Pontiac's full-size Catalina and Bonneville models.

Originally the GTO was offered as a cost option on the regular "Tempest" model, but it soon gained immense popularity due to its performance capabilities and, in 1966, it became a standalone model. The sales were an immediate success, launching the GTO's journey to American iconic automobile status.

Model illustrated:	1966 389 Pontiac GTO 2-Door Hardtop
Power:	360 hp
Engine:	389 cu.i. (6,375 cc) naturally aspirated 4-barrel carb V8 gasoline with RWD
Weight:	3,445 lbs / 1,563 kg
0-60:	7.9 seconds
Top Speed:	121 mph
Numbers Produced:	96,946 (for 1966 model year GTOs)

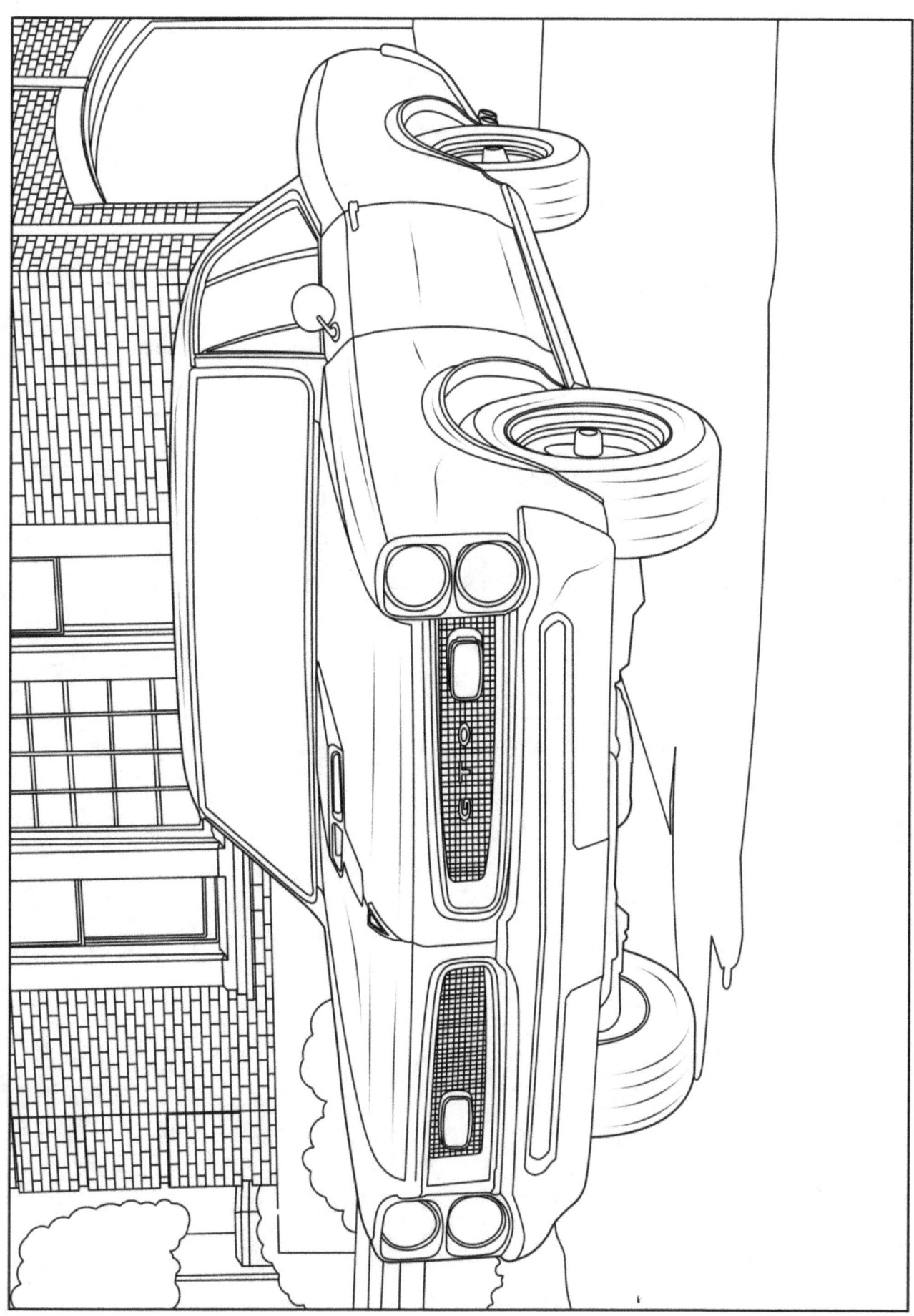

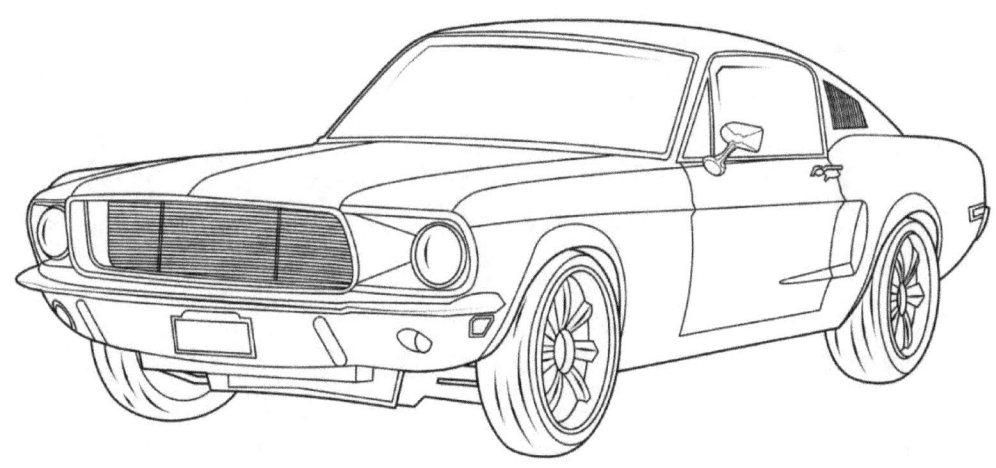

Ford Mustang Fastback GT (1964-Present)

For the past 50+ years American car enthusiasts have had a love affair with Detroit's favorite pony car. Now in its sixth generation — and with an electric SUV now also sharing the nameplate - the Mustang spawned a totally new, extremely cool design in an affordable motor vehicle. Offering a body choice between highly stylized coupé or convertible — with performance and handling to match — the Mustang became, at launch, the most desirable of pony cars (except maybe not the '90s Mustangs!).

Ford bosses initially forecast 100,000 sales a year. But it was such a hit with the American car-buying public that no less than 400,000 units found homes in the first year, rising to a million by the end of year two. The Mustang was so immensely popular that Ford's competitors also wanted a slice of the action. The Chevy Camaro, Pontiac Trans Am Firebird, Plymouth Barracuda and AMC Javelin all had great model offerings and came close, but never really threatened the king.

Often considered to be the single most famous of all Mustangs is the Highland Green 1968 Ford Mustang 390 GT 2+2 Fastback (pictured), driven by Frank Bullitt in the silver screen's most iconic car chase. Over the years the Mustang has become the automotive symbol of American style and remains one of the most highly regarded cars in history.

Model illustrated:	1968 Ford Mustang 390 GT 2+2 Fastback
Power:	425 hp
Engine:	390 cu.i. (6,384 cc) naturally aspirated V8 4-barrel carb gasoline RWD
Weight:	3,347 lbs / 1,518 kg
0-60:	5.9 seconds
Top Speed:	130 mph
Numbers Produced:	10,000,000+ (across all generations)

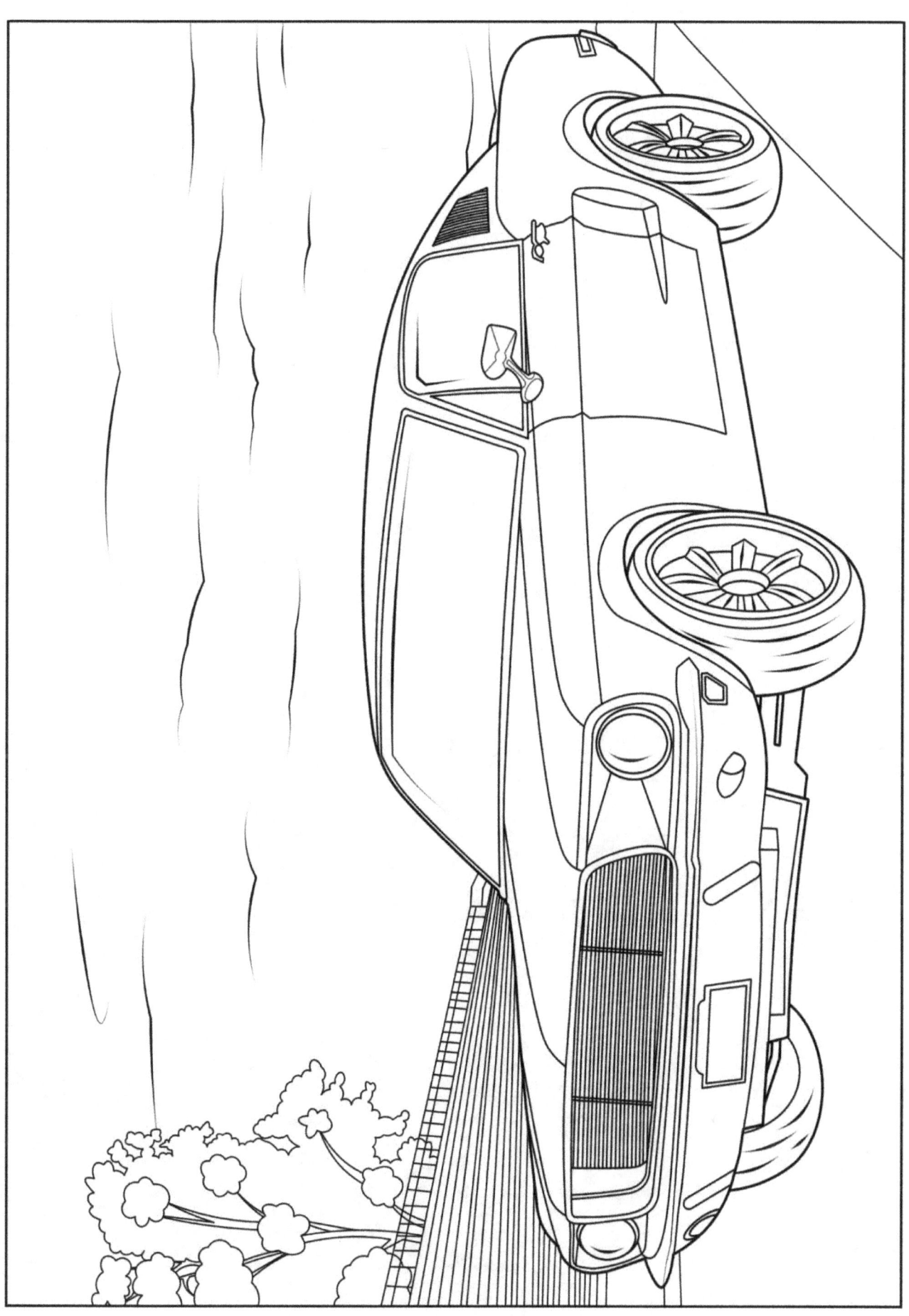

Bucking the trend: the boxy SUV that just kept on getting bigger.

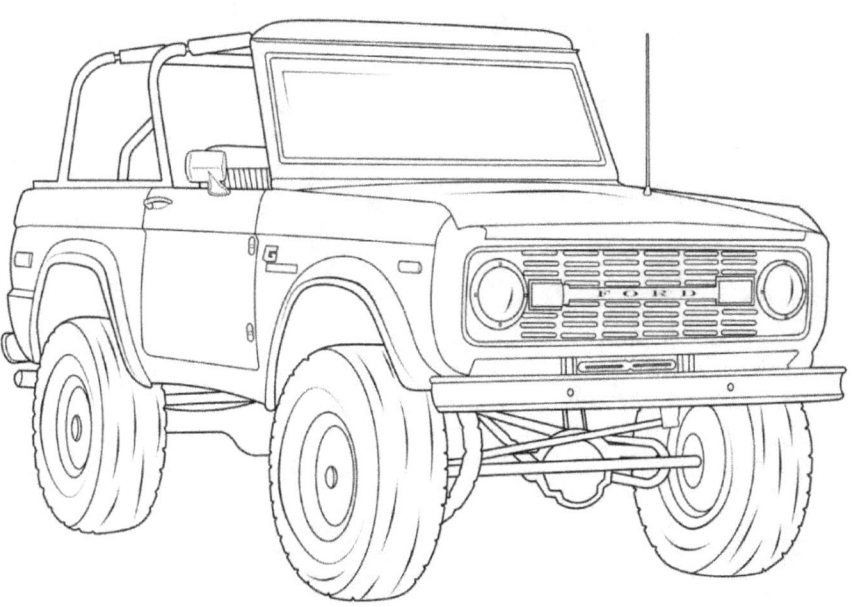

Ford Bronco (1965–1996)

While it may not be the most ground-breaking car in this book, and certainly not the best looking, what the Ford Bronco lacks in style and innovation is certainly made up for by its charm and character. Originally competing against the Jeep CJ-5 and the International Harvester Scout, the Bronco was the first sport utility vehicle to be marketed by Ford. It had its own compact chassis design and offered a heavy-duty driving experience like no other car in its class – as befits a vehicle whose name means "rough, unbroken horse".

First-generation Broncos were equipped with a 170-cu.i. inline-6 which offered 105 hp delivered to all four wheels. Some considered its looks boxy, but its simplicity set the stylistic groundwork for the second generation Bronco arriving in 1978. Significantly bigger, it bucked the trend for more compact SUVs that drank less fuel – a reaction to the 1973 oil crisis. Somehow this worked for the public, and the Bronco went from strength to strength. With its three-door body styling and a lift-off rear hardtop, these second-gen Broncos began competing with Chevy K5 Blazers, Dodge Ramchargers and Jeep Cherokees.

Third and fourth-generation Broncos continued the theme, until the fifth generation brought with it significant changes including considerably different body styling. However, despite big advances in safety and more aerodynamic lines, there could be no escaping the declining interest in 2-door SUVs. In 1996 the decision was taken to discontinue the Bronco to make way for larger SUVs such as the Ford Expedition and Ford Explorer models. But across its very successful 31-year career, the Bronco was a workhorse for many Americans and gained a huge following. Also, its aficionados have something big to look forward to again – a modern-day Bronco is soon to become a reality.

Model illustrated:	1965 Ford Bronco
Power:	105 hp
Engine:	170 cu.i. (2,781 cc) n/a inline six-cylinder with 4WD (Four-Wheel Drive)
Weight:	3,197 lbs / 1,450 kg
0-60:	20 seconds
Top Speed:	80 mph
Numbers Produced:	1,148,926 (across all generations)

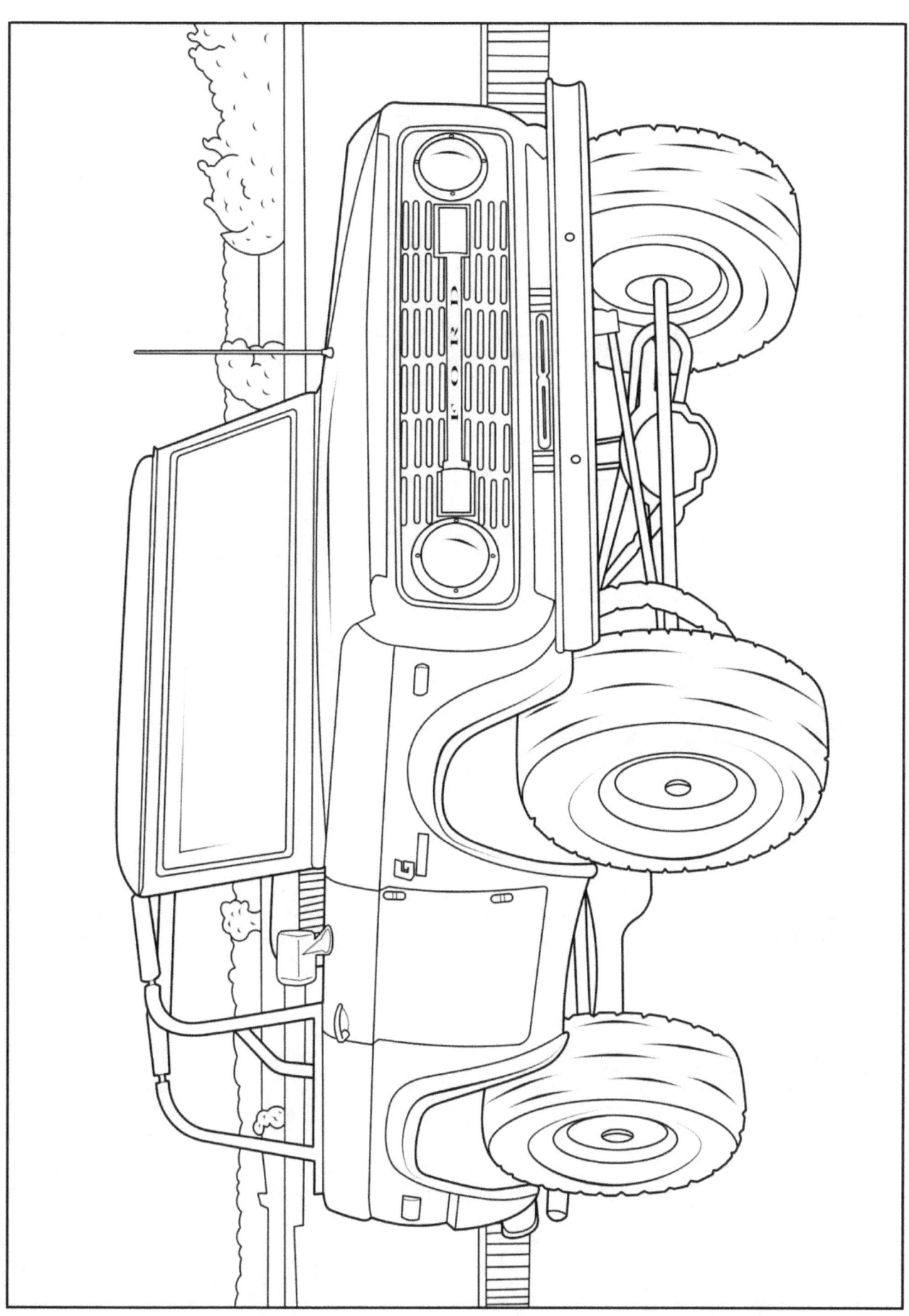

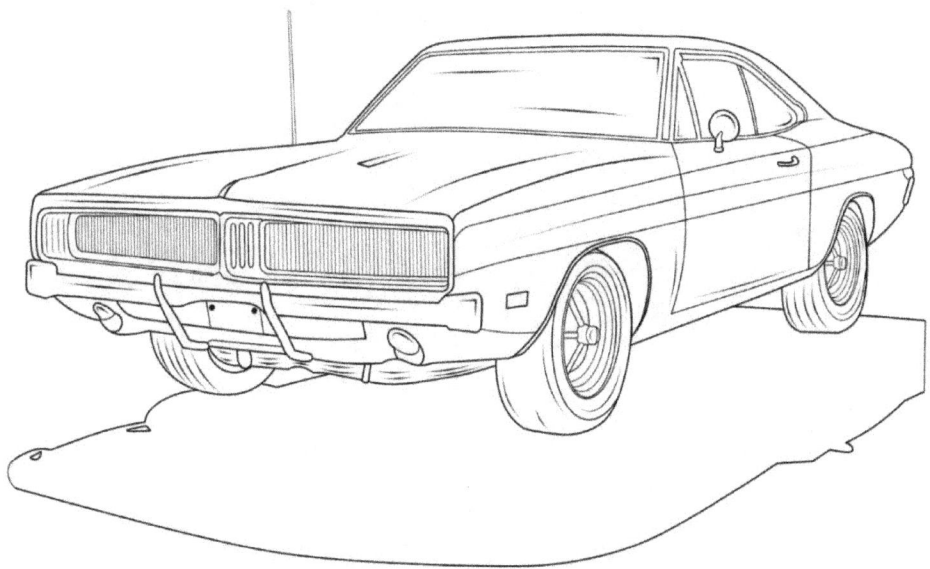

Dodge Charger (1966-1978, 1981-1987, 2005-Present)

For many, even mentioning the name "Dodge Charger" immediately conjures up memories of the "General Lee" from the Dukes of Hazzard jumping over a large ravine, or even a sinister looking '68 R/T with a big block 440 cubic-inch V8 engine under the hood being chased by Frank Bullitt's Mustang – two of the most prominent Chargers in television and cinematic history.

The Charger concept first started life in 1964 as Dodge's response to the enormously popular Plymouth Barracuda and Ford Mustang that were dominating the pony car market. Expectations were high and, eager to make its name on the NASCAR circuit, the first-generation Charger soon proved to be a dominant force. In 1966, its first production year, Chargers won 14 races in the series. And racing success translated well into strong sales figures, fulfilling Dodge's "win on Sunday, sell on Monday" mantra.

The most iconic Charger was the second-generation model produced from 1968-1970. Despite having identical mechanical underpinnings, the gen twos received a complete aesthetic makeover. With seriously cool gen-one features such as hidden headlights in the electric shaver grille they added Coke Bottle styling with integrated trunk spoiler. With its revised looks the Charger could compete toe-to-toe with the 'Cudas and 'Stangs.

Model illustrated:	1969 Dodge Charger R/T 440
Power:	375 hp
Engine:	440 cu.i. (7,206 cc) naturally aspirated big block V8 with RWD
Weight:	3,792 lbs / 1,654 kg
0-60:	6 seconds
Top Speed:	123 mph
Numbers Produced:	231,000+ (second-generation models)

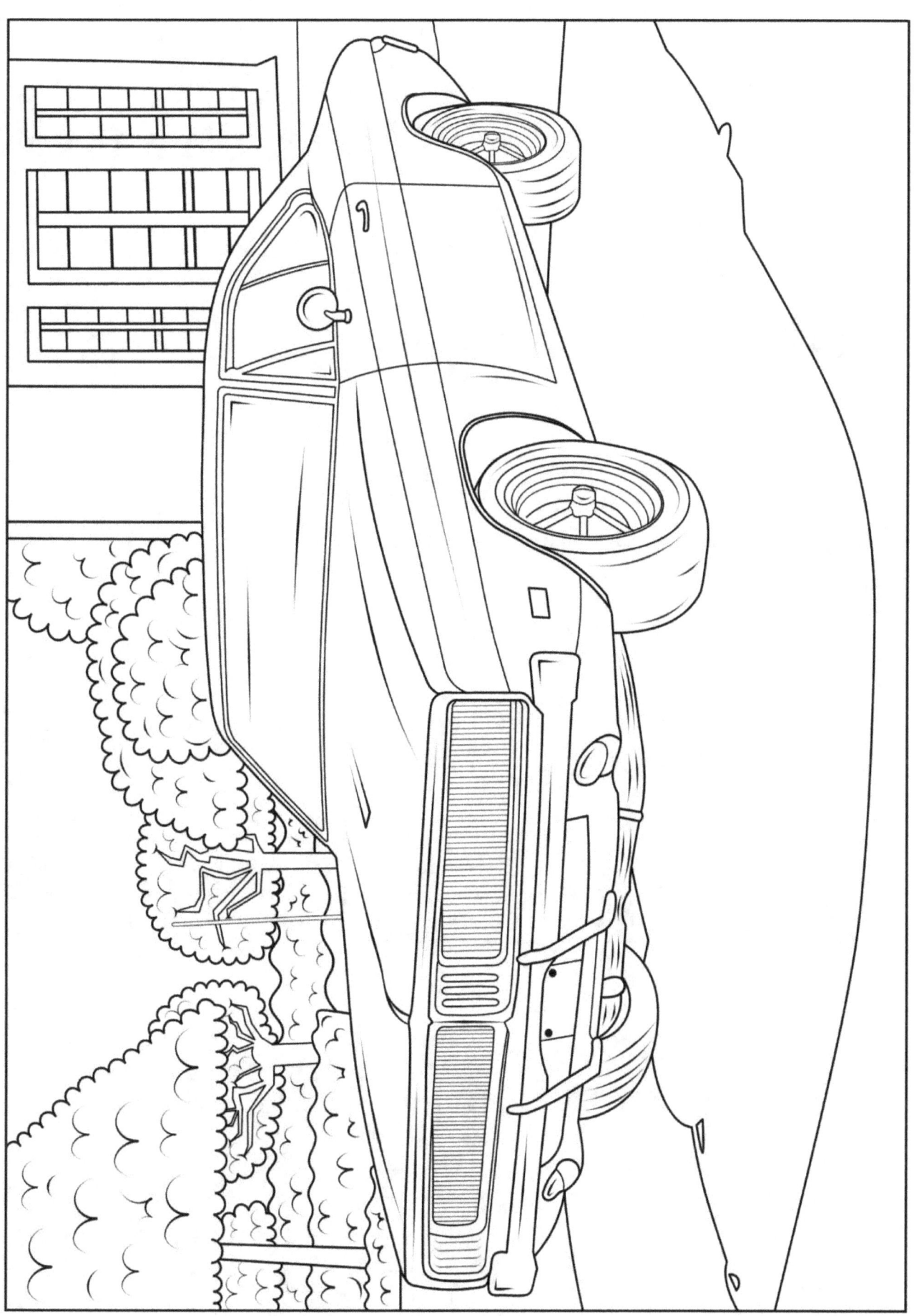

The 6-million-sales car rushed in to grab a slice of Mustang's muscle market.

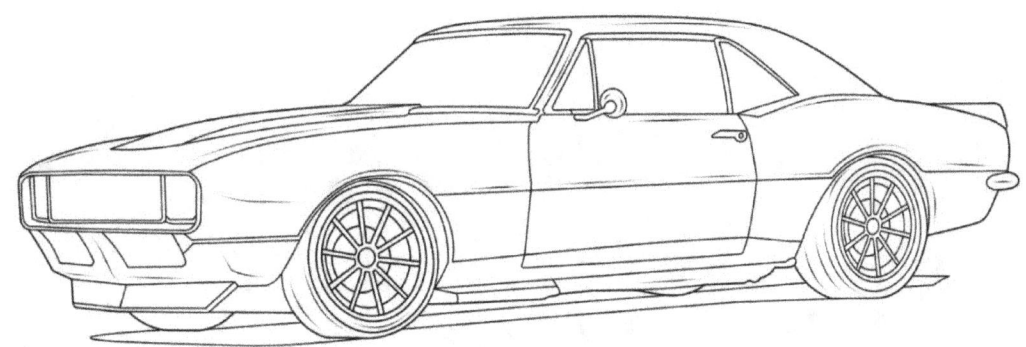

Chevrolet Camaro (1966-2002, 2009-Present)

The massive sales success of Ford's Mustang caught everyone else off guard. So, the Chevrolet Camaro was a rush job. They wanted to get it into production fast to grab a slice of this new and rapidly evolving pony car segment of the market. Chevrolet's rear-engine Corvair wasn't going to cut it, nor did its Chevy II Nova have sufficient presence to compete against Ford's new automotive rock star.

Ultimately the same car as a Pontiac Firebird under the skin, the Chevy Camaro managed to get to the showrooms for the fall of 1966 as a 2+2 hardtop or convertible. Buyers could choose between a straight-six or V8 engine under the hood. First-year sales were reasonable at nearly half those of their main Ford rival: 220,000 vs the Mustang's 480,000.

Now, with six generations and nearly six million sales under its belt, the Camaro has proven to be a heavy influence on US car culture and ranks as a standard bearer for classic American muscle.

Model illustrated:	1967 Chevrolet Camaro RS Super Sport (the "RS" includes the "Rally Sport" option)
Power:	295 hp
Engine:	350 cu.i. (5,733 cc) naturally aspirated small block V8 with RWD
Weight:	3,492 lbs / 1,584 kg
0-60:	6.2 seconds
Top Speed:	118 mph
Numbers Produced:	5,500,000+ (across all generations)

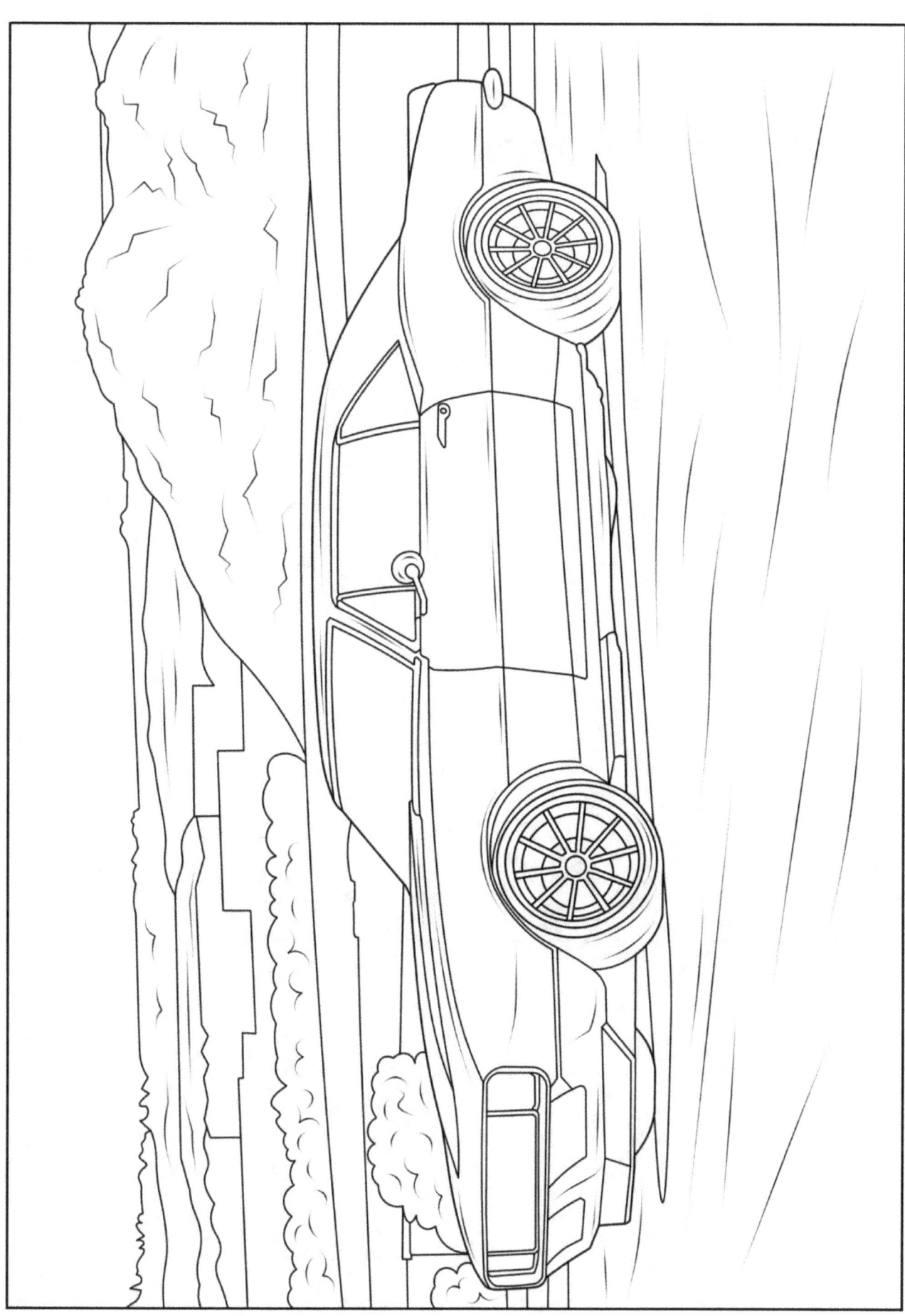

Michael Knight's and the Bandit's choice - a star on the road and silver screen.

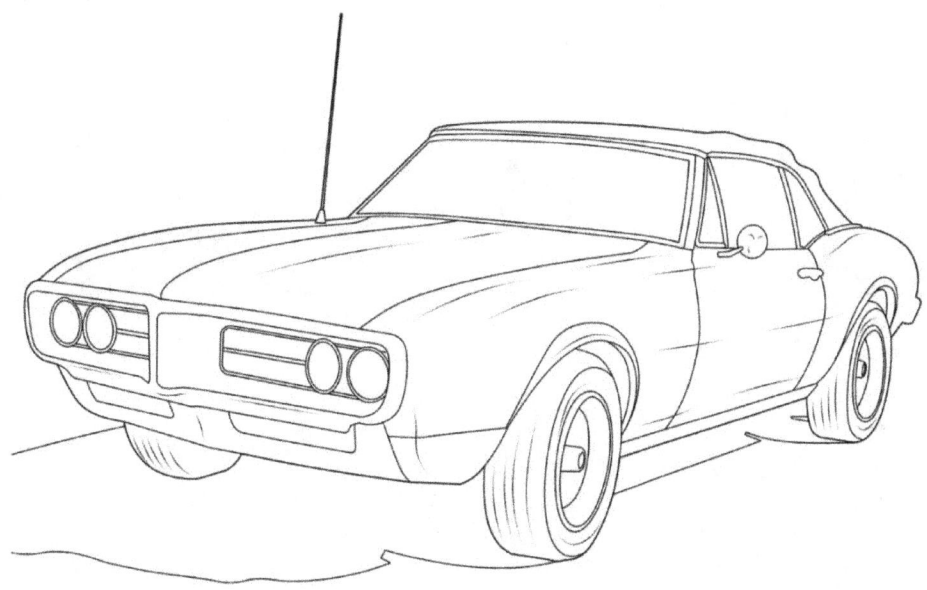

Pontiac GTO (1964-1974, 2004-2006)

Cars don't get any more American than the Firebird, Pontiac's response to the Mustang and Mercury Cougar in the pony car market. The Firebird and its cousin, the Chevy Camaro, shared the same platform.

Named after the incredibly popular Trans Am Racing Series in North America, the Firebird Trans Am showed GM's clear intention to cut itself an even bigger slice of the pony car marketplace. Initially treated to immensely powerful engines, each new generation of Trans Am power plants became a little more muted.

First-gen Firebirds enjoyed the markedly popular "Coke Bottle" styling influences, pronounced front and rear wheel arches and a slim waist. Like its counterparts, the Firebird came in the familiar hardtop and convertible body styles. Engines started with a 3.8-liter straight six and ran up to the range-topping GTO model's 6.6-liter monster sitting proudly under the hood.

The Firebird also scored some reasonably significant TV and film appearances over its four generations. Perhaps most famously it was the choice of Bo "Bandit" Darville in the 1977 movie Smokey and the Bandit – second only to the original Star Wars in box office takings that year! And a little later it also starred as KITT ("Knight Industries Two Thousand") – Michael Knight's artificially intelligent 1982 model from the original Knight Rider TV series. Both screen outings were as iconic as the car itself, and both helped cement the Firebird's ongoing popularity with American car enthusiasts.

Model illustrated:	1968 Pontiac Firebird 350 High Output Convertible
Power:	265 hp
Engine:	354 cu.i. (5,812 cc) naturally aspirated small block V8 with RWD
Weight:	3,492 lbs / 1,584 kg
0-60:	6.4 seconds
Top Speed:	120 mph
Numbers Produced:	277,000+ (first generation from 1969 through 1969)

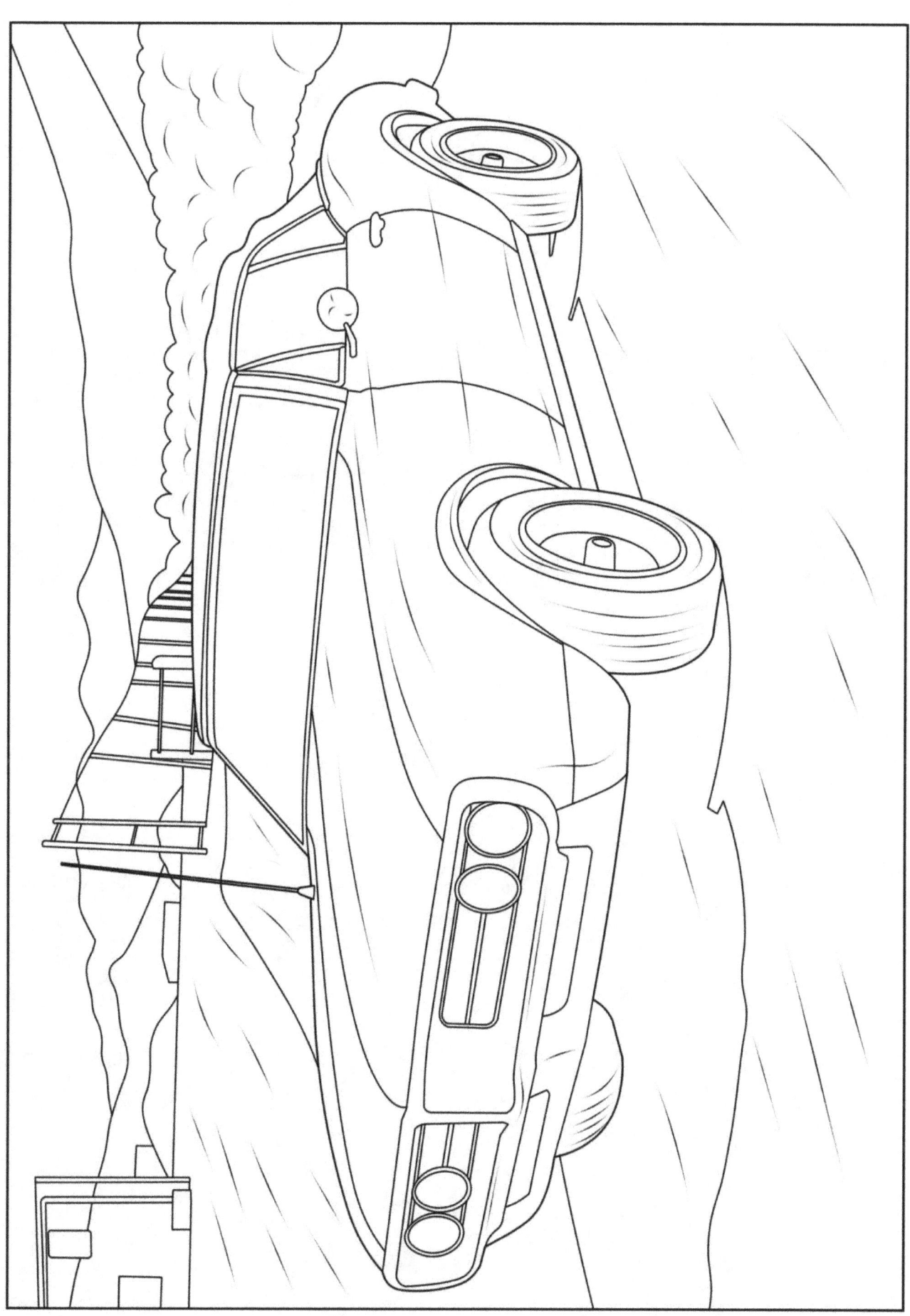

Car of The Year + abundant options = "a car for every American".

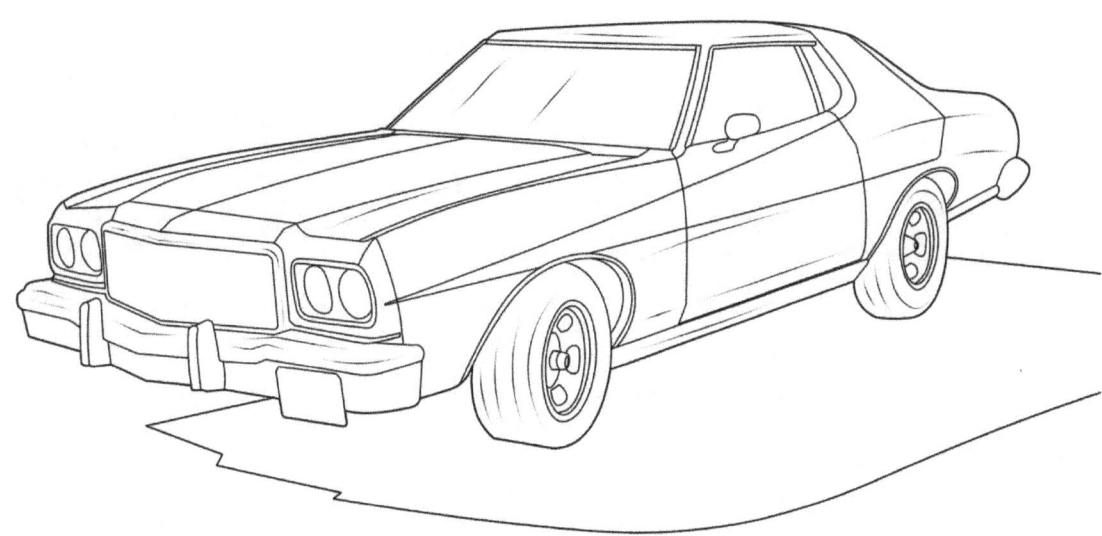

Ford Torino (1968–1976)

Despite its relatively short lifespan of only nine years, the Torino managed to find a place in many American hearts. Originally described as "Ford's newest bright idea", and named after Turin, "the Italian Detroit", the intermediate sized Torino was created to replace the hugely popular Fairlane in the family and executive car sectors.

The Torino was offered with several body styles: two-door fastback, two-door hardtop, two-door convertible; four-door station wagon and four-door sedan. Its wide variety of bodies came with a great choice of engine variants, including 429 Thunder Jet, Cobra Jet and Super Jet engines. So, there was certainly no shortage of options, which appealed to a broad range of customers from families through to style-conscious company execs looking to impress. The Torino was so popular, in fact, that it was Motor Trend's Car of the Year for 1970.

With three reasonably successful generations and featuring prominently in hit movies and TV shows (Gran Torino and Starsky & Hutch respectively), in its many guises the Torino proved to be popular with the American car buying public. However, it was plagued with reliability and corrosion issues, resulting in poor resale values. Over its lifespan the Torino offered a car for everyone – from a sensible family wagon to a powerful muscle car – and everything in between.

Model illustrated:	1976 351 cu.i. Ford Gran Torino 2-Door Hardtop "Striped Tomato"
Power:	255 hp
Engine:	351 cu.i. (5,752 cc) naturally aspirated "Windsor" small block V8 with RWD
Weight:	4,206 lbs / 1,908 kg
0-60:	8.1 seconds
Top Speed:	140 mph
Numbers Produced:	2 million+ (across all three generations)

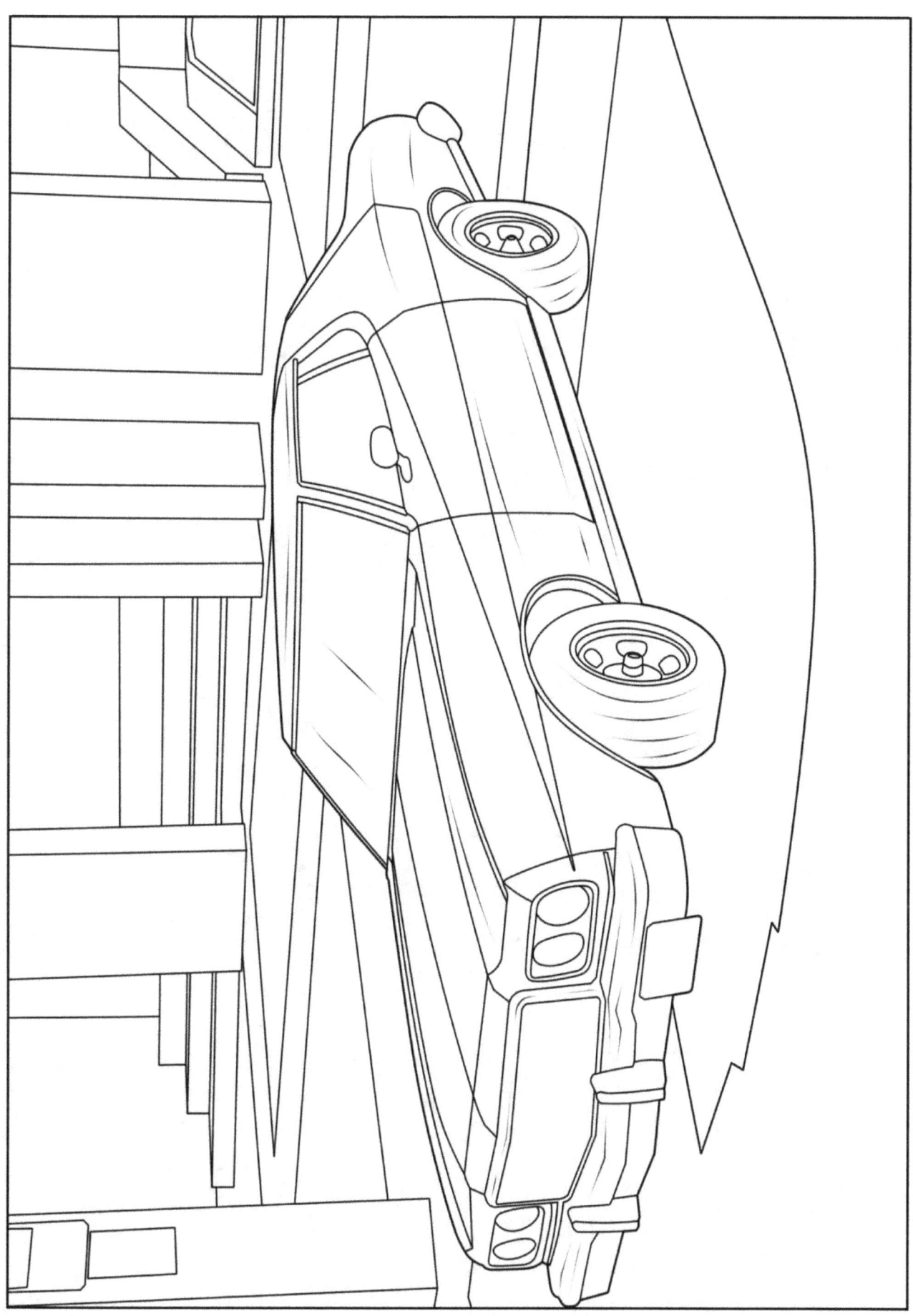

"Cute... or controversial?" Automotive kitsch with an ace up its sleeve.

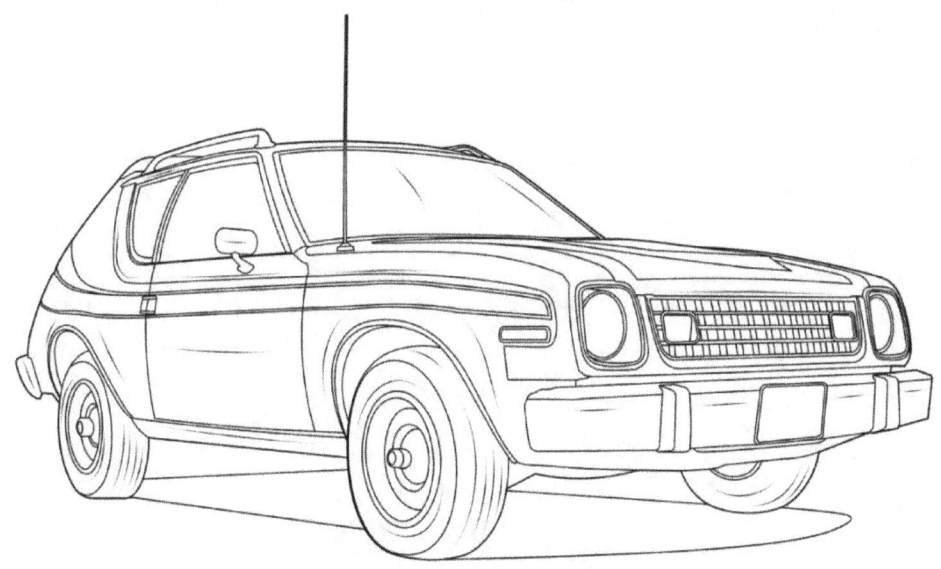

AMC Gremlin (1970-1978)

The AMC Gremlin's design sketch was originally roughed out onto an airplane sick bag, so it was always likely to lead to something a little different or unusual. According to AMC's Chief Designer Dick Teague, it was either going to be "cute or controversial, depending on your viewpoint". The name also held the possibility of negative connotations, a gremlin defined in dictionaries as "a small gnome held to be responsible for malfunction of equipment". AMC's positive spin, however, suggested "a pal to its friends and an ogre to its enemies". Either way, AMC intended it to be the sub-compact of choice for free-thinking Americans.

Fundamentally a truncated AMC Hornet, the Gremlin was squeezed from a compact into the subcompact sector by lopping a full 12 inches off its wheelbase. This made it comparable to the likes of the VW Beetle, the Chevrolet Vega and the ubiquitous Ford Pinto. Engine options started with a 199 cubic-inch inline six, producing 128 hp. An optional upgrade offered a 232-cubic-inch inline six and 145 hp. Also available was an "X" option pack which gave the Gremlin a quasi-muscle car persona. Included in the X package were bucket seats, slotted wheels, Goodyear white-letter tires, body side stripes and a blackened grille. And an ace up the Gremlin's sleeve was played in 1972 with a 304 cubic-inch V8 engine. With 150 hp on tap the V8 Gremlin was good for 0-60 in around 9 seconds and gave a ¼ mile time of 16.8 seconds – quicker than entry-level V8 powered pony cars of the time.

Today, the Gremlin is idolized very much as a piece of 1970s automotive kitsch and good examples are very desirable. It's no wonder the little Gremlin proved to be AMC's second best-selling car: a pal to its friends indeed.

Model illustrated:	1977 AMC V8 Gremlin X
Power:	150 hp
Engine:	304 cu.i. (4,981 cc) V8 gasoline RWD
Weight:	2,824 lbs / 1,281 kg
0-60:	9 seconds
Top Speed:	109 mph
Numbers Produced:	671,475 (across its 9-year production history)

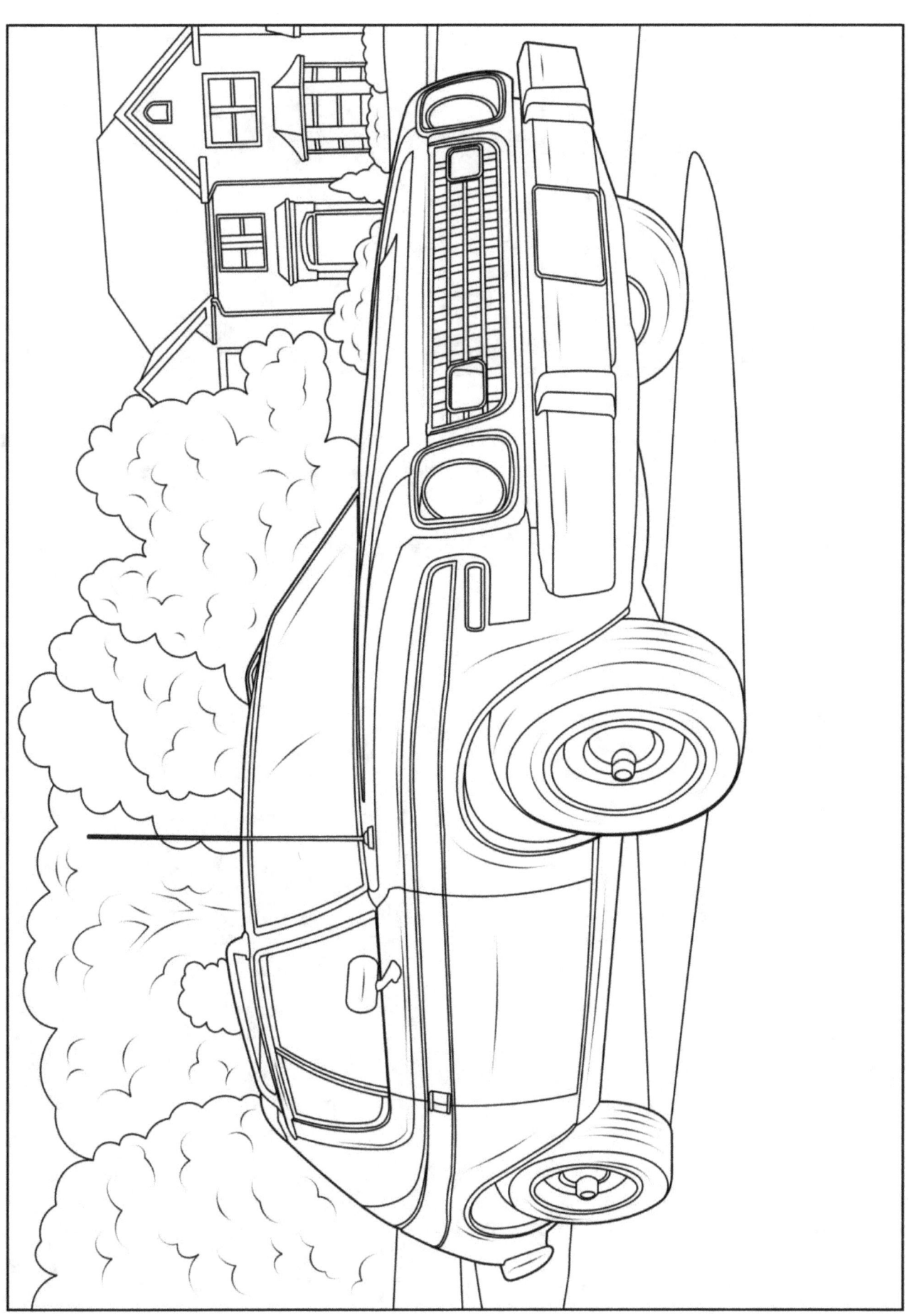

On road or off, a crossover wagon for all seasons.

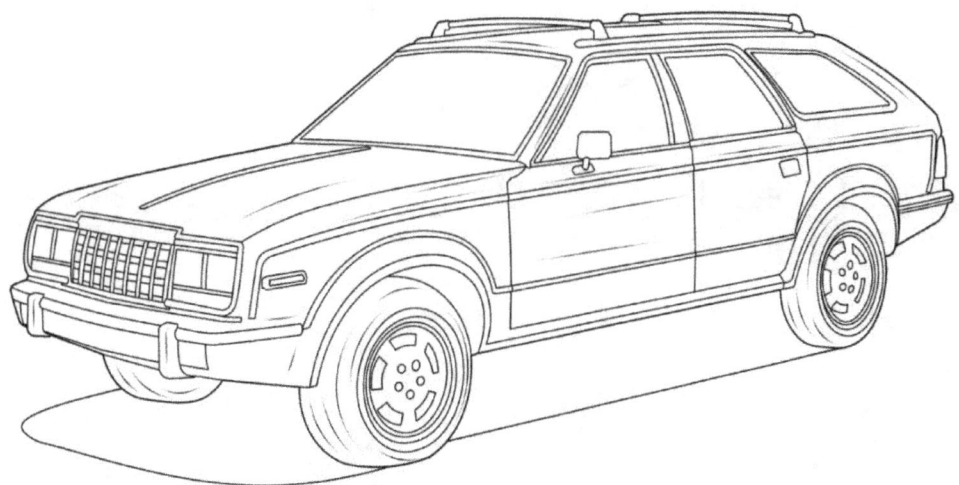

AMC Eagle (1979-1987)

Some Japanese auto manufacturers claim to have built the first "sport utility wagon". But AMC pre-dates these claims with its compact four-wheel drive Eagle, first launched in 1980.

During the 1950s AMC had grown through an amalgamation of well-respected US brands such as Hudson, Nash and Willys. The 1970s brought in the Kaiser Jeep Corporation with its backbone of additional "go anywhere" knowledge. AMC was then regarded as a small company deft enough to exploit special market segments unattended by the giants and it used Jeep's off-road know-how to adapt fundamentally obsolete hardware into successful, road-going crossover vehicles.

Part of the success of the Eagle was due to its cleverly integrated viscous hydraulic single-speed transfer case – often used in today's 4WD vehicles. This enabled the wheels of both front and rear axles to rotate at varying speeds when required, reducing wheel slippage in low traction conditions. Effectively, this was a primitive form of traction control which gave the Eagle competent off-road capability.

Available as a two-door sedan, four-door sedan, two-door liftback, four-door wagon, two-door convertible and also a quirky looking Kammback model, there was a great deal of choice for American drivers seeking extra all-weather driving security. Sales were strong, despite antiquated engine technology. The Eagle was a segment-busting model that defined a new genre still exploited in today's crossover market.

Model illustrated:	1984 AMC Eagle 4.2L Wagon
Power:	115 hp
Engine:	258 cu.i. (4,235 cc) n/a inline-six gasoline RWD or 4WD
Weight:	3,433 lbs / 1,557 kg
0-60:	12.2 seconds
Top Speed:	99 mph
Numbers Produced:	Around 200,000 units across all model years

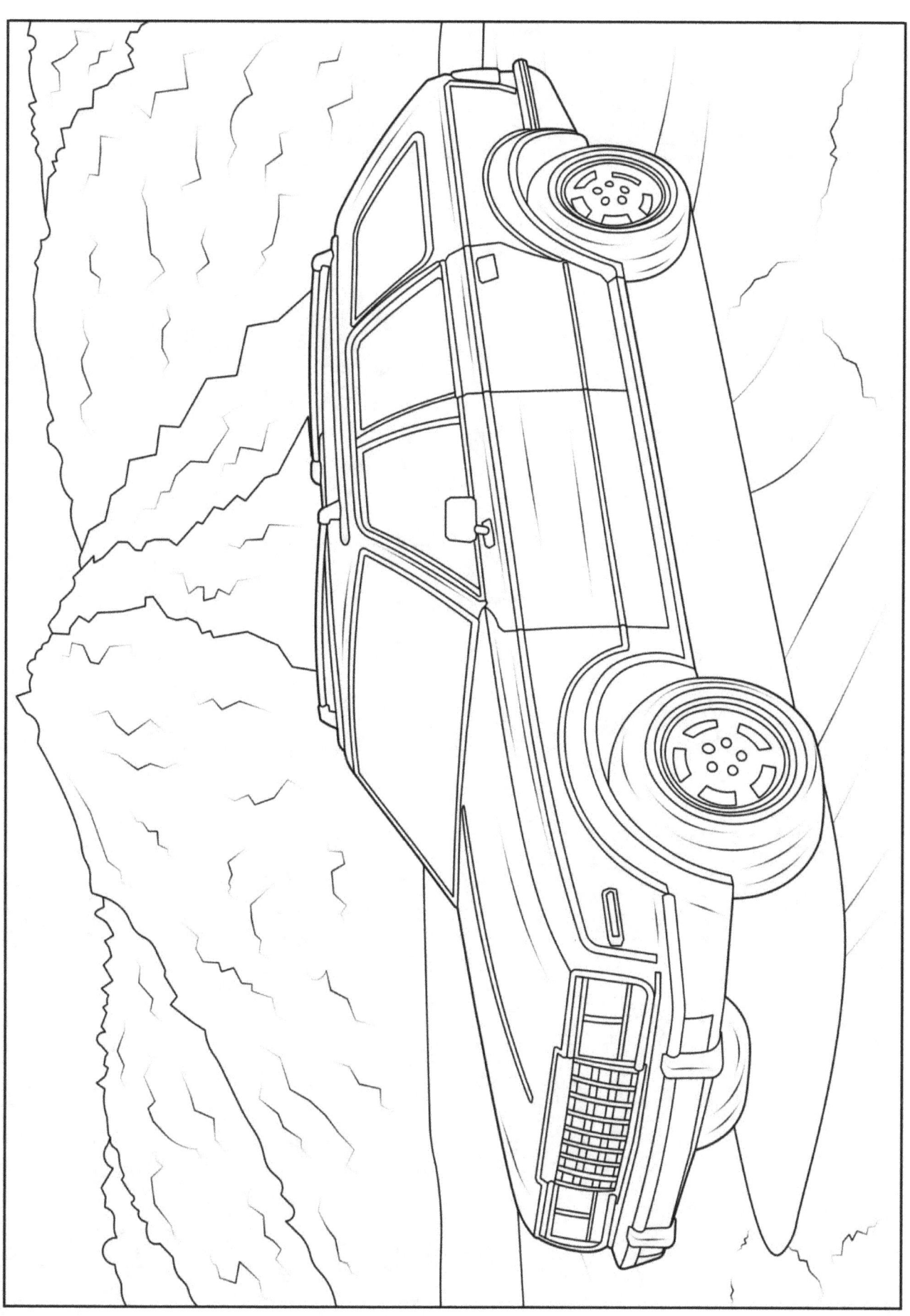

Chrysler dodges death with a perfect suburban family car.

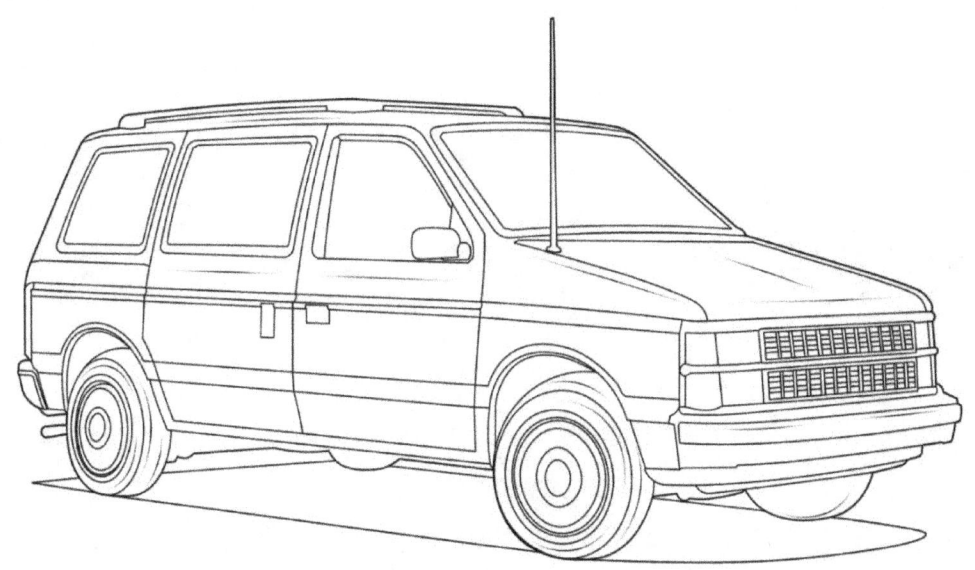

Dodge Caravan/Plymouth Voyager (1983-Present)

In the late 1970s and early 1980s Chrysler had been struggling and was on the verge of bankruptcy. It simply didn't have a strong enough model line up to survive in the automotive industry any longer. So ex-Ford executive Lee Iocacca was given the life-or-death task of creating a car to save the brand. Everyone considered the odds to be heavily stacked against him. But Iocacca proved them wrong when he delivered a massively successful line of minivans branded as the Dodge Caravan and Plymouth Voyager.

The original concept was to provide a good alternative to the safe and sensible station wagon. The minivan – what Europeans now call an MPV (Multi-Purpose Vehicle) or people carrier – would offer significantly more room for its occupants, without much compromise in driving dynamics. Chrysler, and its sub-brands of Dodge and Plymouth, not only managed to save themselves from inevitable demise, but invented a totally new genre of automobile that has proven itself to be a perfect car for suburban America ever since.

Model illustrated:	1983 Dodge Caravan
Power:	101 hp
Engine:	135 cu.i. (2,213 cc) four-cylinder gasoline FWD
Weight:	2,934 lbs / 1,331 kg
0-60:	12.6 seconds
Top Speed:	100 mph
Numbers Produced:	6,000,000 (approx.)

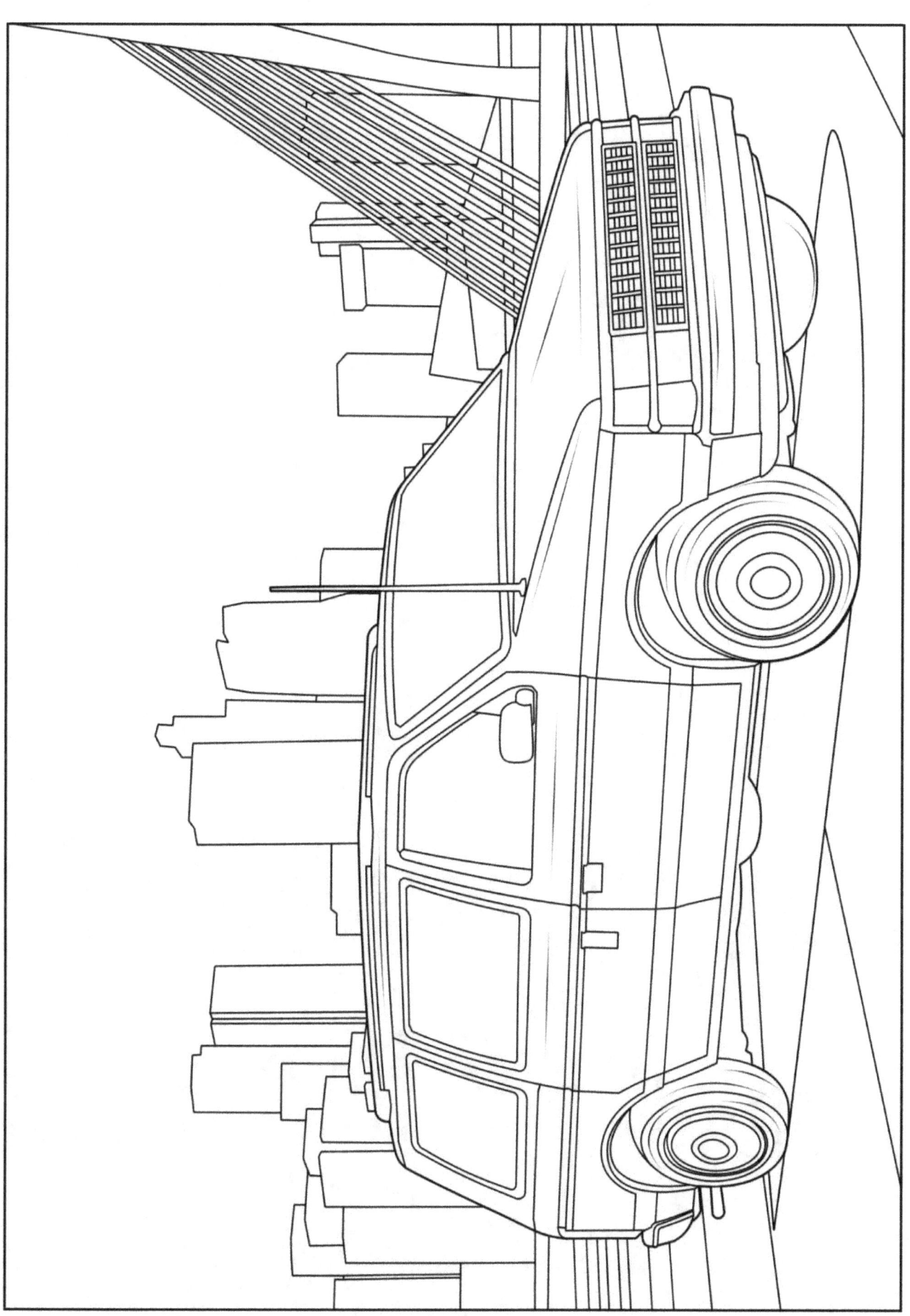

Speed, speed, and more speed - a wild ride built on a shoestring!

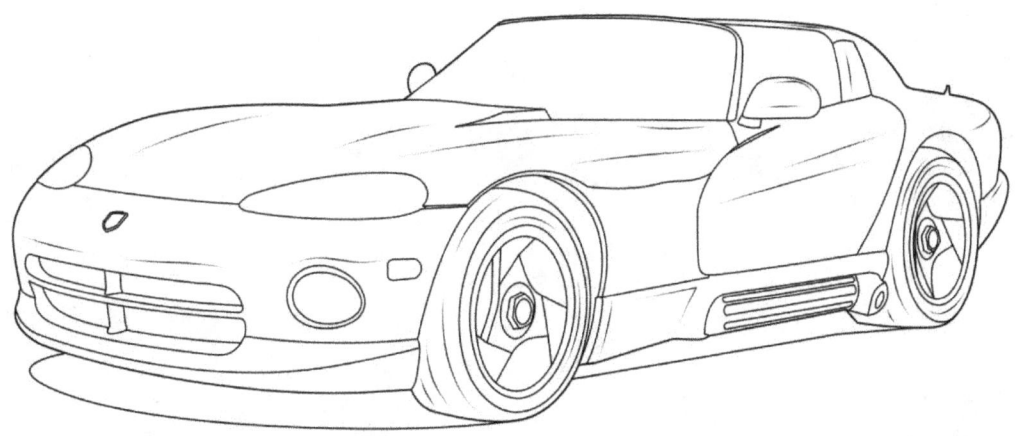

Dodge Viper (1991-2017)

Built on a comparatively shoestring budget of $80m, the Dodge Viper was created to give Americans a "modern-day Cobra" alternative to the Chevrolet Corvette. For far too long adventurous drivers had been limited to just one potent sports car option – or that was the mindset of the Chrysler bigwigs in the 1980s. So, they created the immensely powerful and equally wild Dodge Viper – often referred to as "The Serpent".

The V10 engine sitting under the hood, based on a Dodge truck engine, was upgraded and recast in aluminum by Lamborghini (owned by Chrysler at the time). This absolute monster offered a not insignificant 400 hp and 465 lb. ft. of twist. This kind of power allowed for a 0-60 dash in 4.2 seconds and a top speed of 165 mph. While this top speed may not have been as fast as some of the rival German brands of the era, it really was fast enough when there were no modern-day driver aids such as traction control or ABS. Such aids were considered unnecessary for a performance car and, anyway, their absence saved weight and improved overall performance.

Across the Viper's five generations there were significant developments which added progressively more engine power and a little luxury to what was a purely driver-focused car. For instance, the fifth generation Viper used the same 8.4 liter V-10 as the fourth-generation car, but now produced a massive 640 hp and nearly 600 lb/ft or torque. The Viper was certainly no run-of-the-mill sports car. In the true fashion of the American car industry, the Viper was almost too much to handle.

Model illustrated:	First-Generation Dodge Viper RT/10
Power:	400 hp
Engine:	488 cu.i. (7,990 cc) n/a V10 gasoline with RWD
Weight:	3,280 lbs / 1,488 kg
0-60:	4.2 seconds
Top Speed:	165 mph
Numbers Produced:	31,000+ (across all generations)

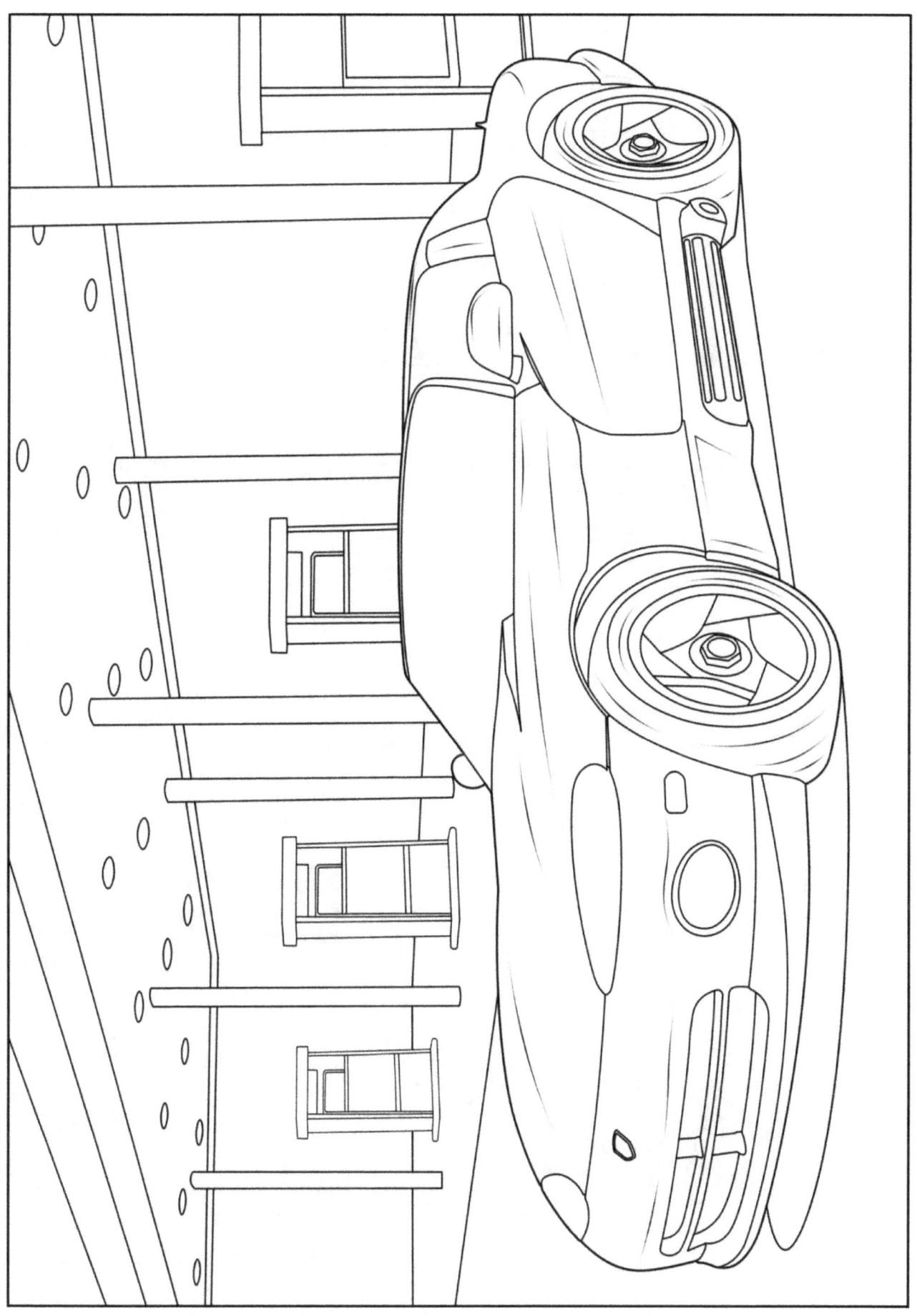

Thanks Arnie, you got us a perfect vehicle for...
American streets.

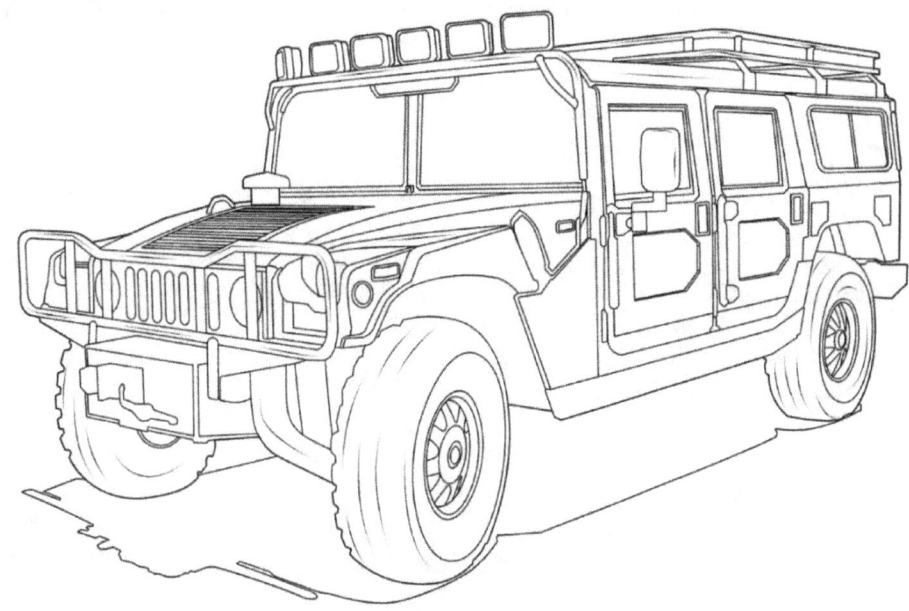

Hummer H1 (1992-2006)

Colloquially known as a "Humvee" (short for "High Mobility Multipurpose Wheeled Vehicle"), the Hummer H1 is a civilized version of the original military M998 Humvee of the 1980s. It had proved an invaluable vehicle in multiple American military situations across the decade running up to the 1990-91 Gulf War.

It may never have come into series production but for the enthusiastic campaigning started by Arnold Schwarzenegger, aimed towards AM General (a subsidiary of American Motors) producing a street-legal version. It was dubbed "the world's most serious 4x4". But in the opinion of discerning enthusiasts, the Hummer's big size, off-road capability and excellent skills at wading through floods made it the perfect option for... American streets!

The H1 came in six main body variants: a soft top convertible, four-door hardtop, Sport Utility Truck and Alpha Wagon. Also available were a two-door pickup and a four-door slantback – a design that was used by its military counterparts in combat. Engines were predominantly Detroit Diesel V8 powered, but a V8 gasoline engine option was also offered during the H1's 14-year history. With its rugged design, powerful engines and go-anywhere capability, the Hummer H1 will forever represent American toughness.

Model illustrated:	2006 Hummer H1 Alpha Wagon
Power:	300 hp
Engine:	403 cu.i. (6,599cc) turbocharged diesel V8 with 4WD
Weight:	8,113 lbs / 3,680 kg
0-60:	12 seconds
Top Speed:	96 mph
Numbers Produced:	11,818 (across full lifecycle)

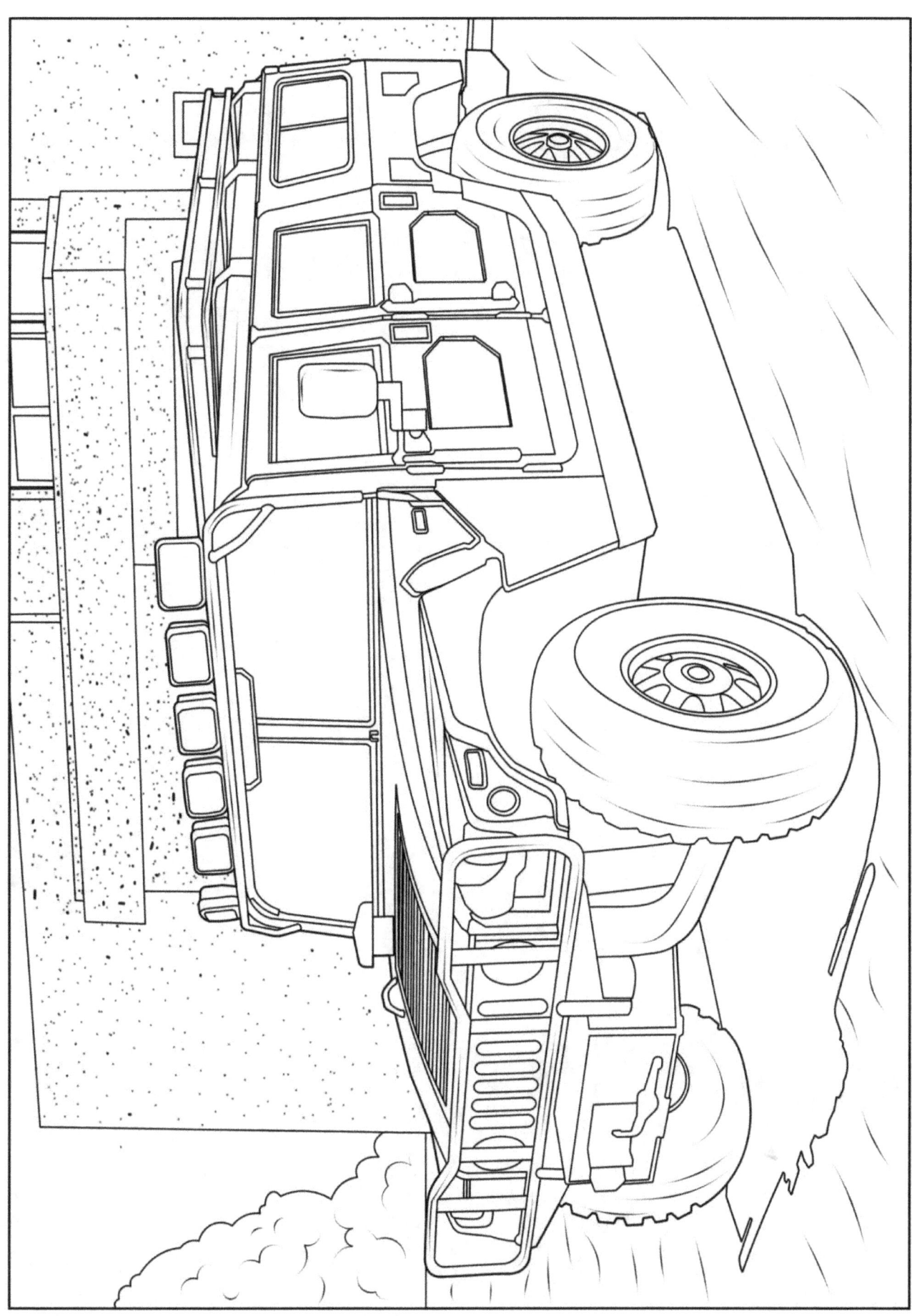

Luxury + speed + saving the planet.
Tesla presents: The Future, now.

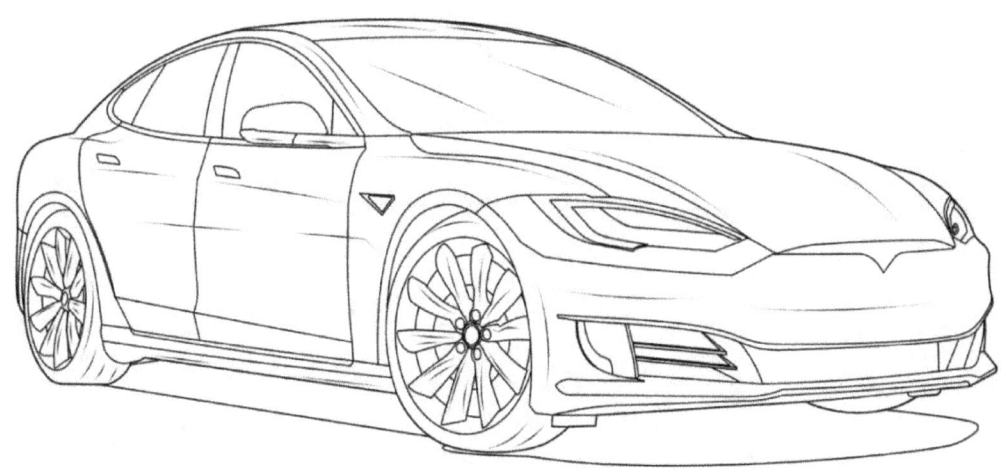

Tesla Model S (2012-Present)

America's significant dominance of the world car industry for much of the 20th century was always going to be difficult to sustain. By the 1980s other manufacturers, especially from Europe and Asia, had caught up significantly in product style, performance, variety, technology, and volume. And they began to cut back the power of US car manufacturers in world markets. Now, Tesla Inc.'s pioneering Model S electric super sedan has successfully reinstated the US automobile industry as a prominent worldwide market force.

Named after Serbian-American inventor Nikola Tesla, Tesla Inc. (formerly Tesla Motors), was founded in 2003 by American entrepreneurs Marc Tarpenning (CFO) and Martin Eberhard (CEO). Initial funding for the company came from a wide variety of sources but, most notably, from the co-founder of PayPal and founder of SpaceX, Elon Musk. Musk invested more than $30 million into the exciting automotive start-up company, becoming first chairman, then CEO. The first car was its fully electric Roadster model in 2008. With a range of 245 miles on a full charge it set unprecedented levels of range for any production electric car. However, at $109,000 it was not necessarily available as a mainstream vehicle.

But with the 2012 Model S, Tesla introduced a car that changed the automotive industry completely. With its pioneering construction, clever design, class leading battery range and supercar levels of performance it single handedly created a realistic electric car market, leaving many competitors stalled on the side of the road with their competing electric vehicles. With the Model S, Tesla has produced something special, perhaps symbolizing the future of the American car industry.

Model illustrated:	2016 Tesla Model S P100D (with Ludicrous Mode)
Power:	671 hp
Engine:	100 kWh Dual electric motors with 4WD
Weight:	5,106 lbs / 2,316 kg
0-60:	2.5 seconds
Top Speed:	155 mph
Numbers Produced:	325,000+ (approximately as per date of publication)

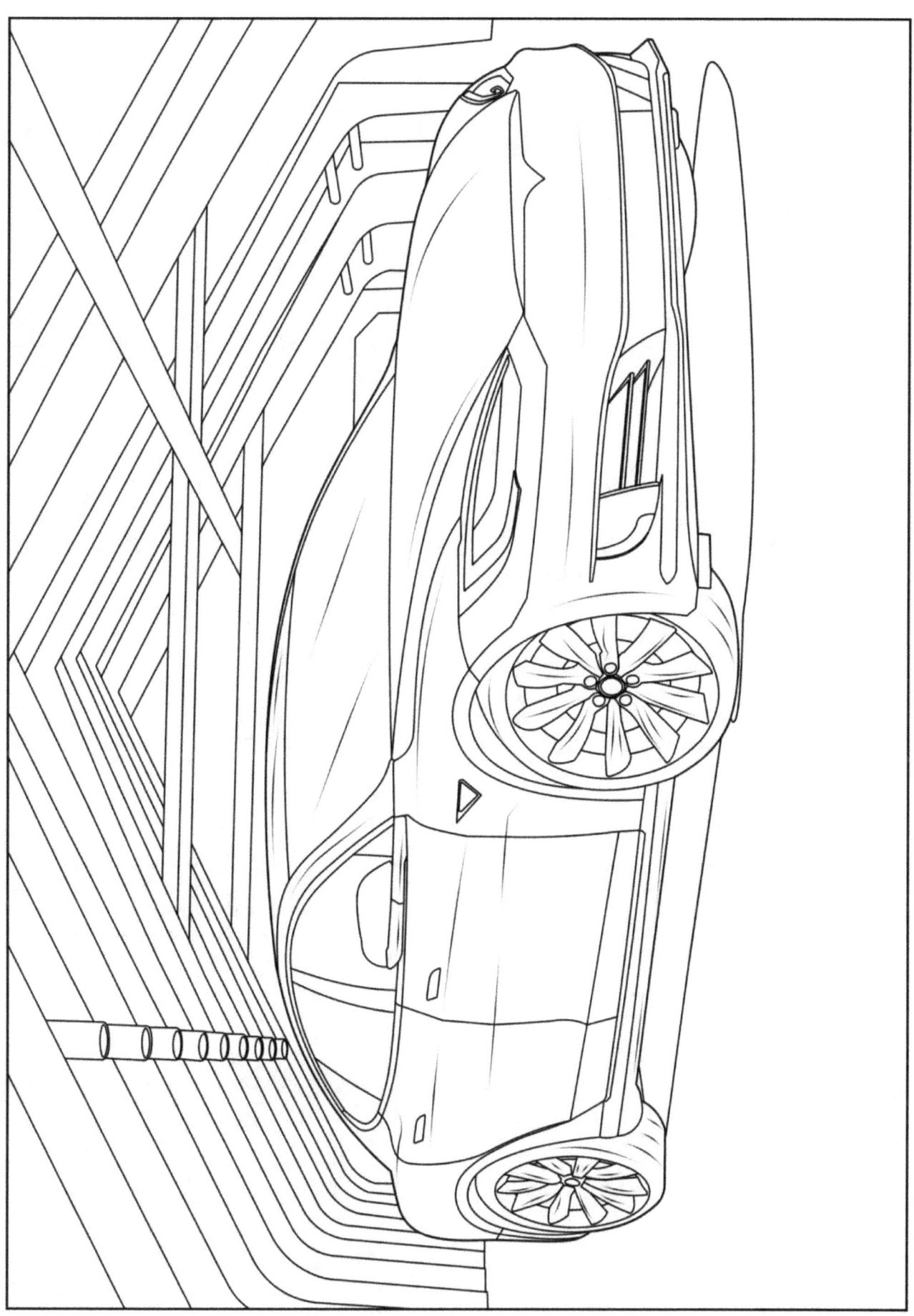

Why not check out the other great titles in this series:

Greatest American Muscle Car Coloring Book – Modern Edition
Includes the following:

- Dodge Challenger SRT Hellcat
- Chevrolet Camaro ZL1
- Ford Mustang Shelby GT 500
- Cadillac CTS-V
- Equus Bass 770
- Ford GT
- Dodge RAM SRT-10
- Jeep Grand Cherokee SRT Trackhawk
- Ford F-150 Raptor
- Dodge Charger SRT Hellcat 'Widebody'
- Chevrolet Corvette Z06
- Dodge Viper

Greatest American Muscle Car Coloring Book – Classic Edition
Includes the following:

- Shelby Mustang GT 500 KR
- Pontiac Tempest Le Mans GTO
- Buick GSX Stage 1
- Ford Mustang Boss 302
- Chevrolet Malibu SS Chevelle
- Dodge Charger R/T SE
- Oldsmobile 4-4-2
- Plymouth Road Runner
- Pontiac Firebird Trans Am
- Shelby Cobra 427
- Chevrolet Camaro IROC-Z
- Chevrolet Corvette 'Stingray'

The World's Most Iconic Cars Coloring Book – Pro Edition
Includes the following:

- Ford Model T
- MINI
- Citroen DS
- Jaguar E-Type
- Volkswagen Beetle
- Mercedes-Benz 300 SL
- Chevrolet Bel-Air
- Toyota 2000 GT
- Porsche 911 Carrera 2.7 RS
- Ferrari LaFerrari
- Lamborghini Miura P400
- Duesenberg Model J
- Aston Martin DB5
- Lamborghini Countach
- Ferrari 250 GTO

The World's Best Hot Hatches Coloring Book – Pro Edition
Includes the following:

- Simca 1100Ti
- Volkswagen Golf GTI Mk1
- Talbot Sunbeam Lotus
- Renault 5 Turbo 2
- Peugeot 205 1.9 GTI
- Lancia Delta Integrale Evolution II
- Renault Clio Williams
- Renault Clio V6 Phase 2
- MINI JCW GP
- Renault Mégane R26.R
- Ford Focus RS500
- Honda Civic Type-R (FK8)

The Ultimate Porsche 911 Coloring Book – Pro Edition
Includes the following:

- First generation 911
- Second generation 'G' Series
- Porsche 911 SC
- Porsche 911 Carrera 3.2
- Porsche 911 964
- Porsche 911 993
- Porsche 911 996
- Porsche 911 997
- Porsche 911 991
- Porsche 911 992

Porsche Specials:
- Porsche 911 Carrera RS 2.7
- Porsche 911 935 'Moby Dick'
- Porsche 911 997 Speedster
- Porsche 911 50th Anniversary Edition
- Porsche 911 R
- Porsche 911 991 GT2 RS

The Greatest American Cars Coloring Book: A Small Favor

Thank you so much for purchasing this 'Greatest American Cars Coloring Book - Pro Edition'. I really hope you enjoyed bringing to life these intricately detailed illustrations and that you appreciated my choice of cars that made it into this book.

Cars are a true passion of mine. I am often thinking about them when I am awake, and I regularly dream about cars when I am sleeping! That's how much I love cars! I also really enjoy creating these books to share with like-minded car lovers around the world. It would mean everything to me if you would kindly share your experience with an honest reflection of your opinion with an Amazon review so others might benefit from your coloring experience. It will help me keep on creating more books in this series for your coloring pleasure.

Thanks again and take care,

Alexander Watts

Come and join the car coloring revolution with Alexander Watts's Car Coloring Club!

Okay, so I see you enjoy learning about great cars. Well, why don't you subscribe to Alexander Watts's Car Coloring Club to make sure you don't miss any exciting new content that I have coming out? Subscribing is easy and fully secure - just get your smart phone out (or ask an adult if you don't have one) and take a picture of the QR code below. It will take you right through to the email subscription page so you don't miss a thing! There will be free coloring giveaways and regular new content. Subscribe now so you don't miss out on the fun!